MAGAZINE ARTICLE WRITING

MAGAZINE ARTICLE WRITING

by

Mary T. Dillon

*How to write and sell
short nonfiction*

Publishers   THE WRITER, INC.   *Boston*

Library of Congress Cataloging in Publication Data

Dillon, Mary T.
  Magazine article writing.

  1. Authorship—Handbooks, manuals, etc. I. Title.
PN147.D54   808'.02   77-8241
ISBN 0-87116-107-9

Manufactured in the United States of America.

Writer 2/79 6897

Contents

Acknowledgments

Portions of the following articles are reprinted with the permission of the publishers:

"Cross-Country Skiing," by Lynn Ferrin. Copyright © 1976 by Ms. Magazine Corp. Reprinted by permission.

"Dry Stone Walls: Building Them to Last," by Julian Fish. Reprinted by permission of The Early American Society, Inc., from *Early American Life* Magazine.

"I Was Told I Had Only Six Months To Live," by Senator Frank Church. Reprinted by permission of William Barry Furlong, from the January 1976 issue of *Good Housekeeping* Magazine. © 1975 by the Hearst Corporation.

"The Man Who Watched 1,500 Late, Late Movies," by Walt Schmidt. Reprinted with permission. © 1975 The Saturday Evening Post Company.

"On the Job: What It Takes for a Woman to Get Ahead," by Claire Safran. Reprinted from *Redbook* Magazine, January 1977. Copyright © 1976 by The Redbook Publishing Company.

"Therapy for Dogs," by Newton F. Tolman. Reprinted by permission from *UpCountry* by permission of the author and Berkshire Publishing Company.

"A Yankee Pilgrim in the Old South," by Blair Sabol. © 1977 by The New York Times Company. Reprinted by permission.

Preface

A writer's work reflects the writer, from selection of subject to presentation of material. What catches *your* attention, what moves and inspires *you*, how *you* react to given situations, will determine what and how you write. Magazine writing is almost certain to extend your horizons and broaden your understanding of people and the world. In the beginning you may decide to concentrate on writing the kind of article you yourself like to read. You will probably reach farther and farther out in your search for subjects as time goes on. But whatever you elect to write about, the writing itself cannot help but mirror your individual interests, reflecting your tastes, prejudices, background and capabilities.

As this is written, there is every reason for anyone interested in breaking into the field of magazine article writing to feel optimistic. With several thousand publications geared to the tastes, concerns, and needs of persons of all ages and every kind of circumstance in life, anyone with something to say (or simply an itch to write and be published) and capable of setting one word down after another in orderly fashion should be able to find a market for his or her work.

Like any professional field of work, writing and selling magazine articles involves the use of special tools and techniques. No one questions the need for specialized training and a period of apprenticeship in preparation for the professions of law, medicine, nursing, or teaching. But for some reason, many people look on writing for profit as something that, if they attempt it at all, they should be able to succeed at immediately. If their first efforts meet with rejection, they give up, and, concluding they have no talent, they try no more. Actually, the ability to produce salable articles depends upon a number of other factors, in addition to writing talent, and these can be learned. We shall examine those other factors in forthcoming chapters of this book.

—Mary T. Dillon

MAGAZINE ARTICLE WRITING

~ 1 ~

Learning Your Craft

The years I have spent at an editorial desk have convinced me that many people—the young and the mature—long to write for the magazines they read so avidly and often have good article ideas that they don't know how to develop into finished form. Yet they often do not realize that article writing is, to a large degree, a learned skill. Certainly there are individuals who are able to express their thoughts on paper with great ease. But for every well-established and successful writer who has that natural facility with words, there is almost certainly another who must labor to get thoughts down on paper clearly and comprehensibly.

Facility with words does not in itself make a successful writer. Nor is the absence of that facility a fatal lack for a writer with a lively curiosity and a willingness to work hard. In writing, as in many other fields of endeavor, one learns by doing. Each article tackled teaches its writer something. There is as much to be learned—perhaps more—from failures as from successes. Editorial comments on a rejected article can be invaluable, but they probably won't be offered unless the piece is a "near miss" and the editor sees in it some promise for the future. Instead of resenting criti-

3

cism, be grateful for it, and pay close attention to critical comments and editorial suggestions. If the editor pinpoints a weakness—"lack of specifics," for example—or asks leading questions: "How many?" "How did she look?" "What did he say?" "Where did they go?"—make sure to remedy all the noted omissions before submitting a revision.

Using your senses

When an editor asks questions like these, he is suggesting obliquely that you have left readers without the clues they need to form clear impressions of the people and places that figure in your article. Concrete detail, specific quotes, colorful description—the very same sort of material the fiction writer uses—are what the article needs to give it impact. You will be surprised to discover how much a piece improves when you answer those editorial questions, inserting the requested detail and expanding the sections the editor considered inadequate. You will find that you are putting down on paper bits of information that were stored in your memory and were, in fact, a part of your article, but that, up to now, you neglected to share with the reader. You unconsciously "read into the piece" those missing bits and pieces; it took the editor's objective eye to pinpoint the omissions for you.

An honest, clear-eyed evaluation of your own work in the light of whatever critical comments have accompanied its rejection by one or more editors may reveal a number of things. Eventually, you need to develop a capacity for self-criticism so that you yourself will be able to spot weaknesses in an article and remedy them before sending the manuscript out for editorial consideration. A checklist can be helpful. Ask yourself if you have carried the research far enough and used your research material to the best advantage. How about the lead? Is it the very best you can develop? Will it unfailingly grasp the reader's attention and make him want to read on? If not, the lead you have used is not good enough, for all your efforts are useless if the article is not read.

Ask yourself if the subject you have chosen is one that will appeal to many readers. Would *you* pick up a magazine in order to read an article on birding, for example, or on fish farming or modern highway construction? Very possibly not, *unless* the title and first paragraph were sufficiently arresting to grasp and hold your attention. What can be done to your article to make its specialized subject matter compellingly interesting to the average reader?

Another question to include in your checklist: Is this the kind of article you are best equipped to write? It may be that you have been limiting yourself too much to one type of piece when you could be more successful with something quite different. As detailed in later chapters, subjects can be presented in many different ways. Perhaps you should try a radical reshaping of the text, using the same set of facts, but presenting them in another way, perhaps aiming at another sort of audience. The birding story, for example, would be done quite differently for readers of *Audubon* or *Natural History* than for *The Reader's Digest*'s mass audience.

In assessing your own capabilities, think back to high school and college days. Did you often have poems published then, or was your interest directed to the school or college newspaper and the reporting of academic, sports or social events on campus? If you loved poetry (and presumably still do), your talents probably lie in the area of descriptive writing, the sort of evocative piece that appeals to our love of nostalgia, depending heavily on the well-remembered, graphically described scene and demanding skillful and original writing to put it across effectively.

"Nostalgia is big these days," I heard an editor remark not long ago. When well done, the nostalgic piece is reliably salable, most often when the material provides, in addition to its nostalgic appeal, some clear-cut link with the present. A seventy-year-old's recollections of long-ago boating experiences made a delightful piece for *Yachting Magazine,* in a good-humored record of long-past events that combined nostalgia and laughter for an audience whose empathy could be assumed. The article, originally written with a large-circulation magazine in mind, found its perfect market, thanks to writer Mildred Wohlforth's perseverance in submitting the manuscript until final acceptance.

If you believe there is value in what you have written (and you shouldn't send out anything you don't believe in), then you will do well to keep trying, picking your targets carefully, and always attempting to offer the material to magazines with whose general tone and point of view it seems most compatible.

Bear in mind that the way you write may be more important than what you choose to write about. Your potential audience, the kind of piece you have undertaken, the amount of research you have done, all will obviously affect both your writing and its chances for acceptance. But unless you take time to rewrite and polish your work, seeking always to refine what you have written and to find new, fresh ways of expressing ideas, cutting extraneous words and paragraphs, eliminating clichés—unless you do the hard work that is the final phase of writing, you're not likely to make many sales.

Rewriting *is* essential. It is good procedure to do the first draft in the white heat of your enthusiasm for the idea, then put the manuscript aside for at least two weeks. (Mark Twain is said to have stored unfinished manuscripts whenever his "tank ran dry," sometimes letting them "mature like cheese," as he put it, for months or years before going back to them again.) In the interval, you will find other work to concentrate on so, when you come back to it, the first draft will be more or less new to you. It may surprise you to discover how much of what you wrote a few weeks ago now seems off-center, tangential to the subject. Run a firm pencil line through the unnecessary paragraphs. If a gap is left, a sentence or two can be added for transition. Or it may be best to rearrange the paragraphs to lead the reader along briskly and hold his or her interest to the end.

Pace, sound, rhythm

Pace is undeniably important. Try to make every sentence and paragraph count. (The news magazines provide good models for this, as docs any good daily paper.) If, as you read and reread what you have written, you find there is one point at which your mind wanders, consider whether there may not be a repetition there, a "soft spot" of some kind that needs either to be cut or reworked. Read your manuscripts aloud, and learn to listen as well as look for weak points in your text. Sometimes they are easier to hear than to see.

It would be difficult to overemphasize the importance of listening to what you have written. There should be a cadence in your sentences, but not a monotonous, repetitious rhythm to them. The rhythm should be lively, with longer and shorter sentences alternating and paragraph breaks coming not too far apart.

Although you may not be conscious of doing so, you will want to adapt the rhythm of your prose to the article's subject matter. Edwin Newman did this effectively in his article entitled "New York Without Apologies" (*Saturday Review,* January 10, 1976), in which he caught, in the very sound of the sentences, the nervous, choppy, exciting beat of the debt-ridden metropolis that is home to him:

> New York City is not the Garden of Eden, paved over. But cities have reasons for existing; they serve certain purposes. Thus New York. It may be mismanaged; it may be bloated, ugly, polluted, crowded, run-down, blotched by poverty and a citadel of iniquity. It is also a land of opportunity, beautiful, diverse, energetic and whimsical—where else could action take the form of 23 drawbridges being left open? It did not become what it has because a band of urban conspirators decided to use it to dominate and humiliate the rest of the nation. It is part of the United States, and the United States would be unimaginable without it. . . . All things good do not flow from this city, but neither do all things evil.

Don't be afraid to cut. Economy of language is or should be your constant goal. An article needs to cover a lot of ground in the least possible number of words, compressing and clarifying thought, not digressing far from the main theme. Most people don't naturally write (or talk) this way; rewriting and cutting are what accomplish that tightness and clarity you are aiming to achieve, producing in the text the indefinable tension, the "sparkle" that catches the reader and holds him to the end.

Rewriting involves more than reshaping. Again, let me urge you to *listen*—critically—to what you have written. Does if sound right? Do the stresses come in the right places, with enough variety to relieve the reader from boredom?

Alexander Pope went on for hundreds of pages using the same pattern of stresses. Longfellow's lulling cadence is unmistakable. But our twentieth-century ears are attuned to a broken, almost conversational style. Avoid stodgy, lifeless prose. Make your sentences march and occasionally sing. The way the article is written may be the deciding factor in the editorial decision on it, and if it is published, may determine whether most readers will finish reading it.

Obviously, it takes longer to rewrite an article than to dash off the first draft. But you'll learn something each time you go over the piece. For example, it may become apparent as you rework your text that the original research was insufficient, and the article therefore seems superficial. It is better for you to discover this yourself than for an editor to point it out in a rejection letter. If you reread your notes, you may find small bits of information, descriptive details, brief quotes, and even usable anecdotes you somehow overlooked in your first reading. The material thus salvaged can be appropriately worked into the manuscript to enliven and enrich the text, giving the manuscript a better chance for immediate acceptance.

It may be helpful to go back to your original sources of information or even to look into a few you overlooked before. Anything you find now that is really pertinent should be inserted. Some of your gleanings may survive only as two- and three-word references or statistics parenthetically noted. This sort of information can give the text a depth and credibility it lacked before. (Remember always to note your sources in case the facts are challenged before or after publication; also, identify in the text the sources of all direct quotes.)

Rewriting may involve a recasting of the lead. Would another opening be more effective? Is the ending right? It's not if it leaves the reader in midair with an unsatisfied feeling. Somehow you should convey a sense of completion at the end, perhaps with a closing paragraph that summarizes the message or restates the main point. Now is the time to have one last look at these two crucially important parts of your article.

There are writers who refuse to do this. They pride themselves on being able to dash off a piece at one sitting at the typewriter and get the manuscript into the mail the same day. This may say something about their typing proficiency but it doesn't impress me, even if occasionally they may sell a short article produced this way. It remains an unwise practice and those who indulge in it are not likely to find many markets open to them. It is perfectly possible to retain the spontaneity of the first draft through several careful revisions, while increasing the overall impact of a piece immeasurably. The process of revising and rewriting differentiates hack writer from professional and the sincere newcomer to the field of magazine writing from the dilettante. So take the time and make the effort to go that second mile. It will pay you dividends in the end.

~ 2 ~

The Modern Magazine Article: A Nonfiction Story

Before starting to write, it may be helpful to pause for a moment and think just what it is you plan to produce. What, exactly, *is* an article in the present-day understanding of the term?

An article may be any one of a number of things, but certainly it is not a term paper, with bibliography and foot-notes, although, like the term paper, the factual article should be based on careful research. It is not the sort of detailed informational report a businessman might prepare for circulation to his associates or a legislator for fellow committee members. Nor is it a news report either, although newspaper reporters persist in thinking that it is. And final-ly, an article is not an essay—neither the formal essay of the 19th-century English prose writers, nor the once popular personal or familiar essay, now unfortunately in decline.

Well, then, what *is* an article? The successful magazine article writer will answer, if he thinks objectively about it, that it comes closest to being a nonfiction story—charac-terized by the same meticulous attention to detail, the same concern for unity ("a story must have a beginning, a middle and an end") that is found in a good short story. The aim must always be to engage the reader's attention at the start and hold it to the end.

Fiction techniques

Short story techniques can be very useful. Magazine article writers will succeed in gaining and holding their readers' attention if the text contains essentially the same elements fiction writers use—the color and sound and scent of the happenings, the recorded reactions of the writer or of his protagonist, as picked up and synthesized through the senses. The writer must help the reader see the scene against which the article is set, hear the sounds of what is taking place, smell the sea—or the spruce woods or the scent of honeysuckle on the warm evening air. Without this sort of evocative detail, the reader stands apart, uninvolved and unconcerned; the article fails to "grab" him, as editors sometimes say. For this reason magazine editors work constantly to wrest from their writers the small detail, the quick, telling quote, the additional tidbit of information that will give immediacy, conviction, empathy to the text.

Not only must the scene be set, but the characters—i.e., any people who figure importantly in the story—must be brought to life by means of careful description and painstaking care in the reproduction of their speech. The reader's sympathy and interest can thus be enlisted and his attention held to the article's end. Bits of dialogue and well-chosen descriptive detail will do the trick, enabling the reader to visualize the setting and to hear the voices of the people involved.

Granted, magazine article writers work within strict limitations of space. They must present—in language at least as economical as is required of the fiction writer—the characters in the piece and the essential background of the events. No word can be wasted; every detail should contribute to the whole. The reader, with no background of information, needs help in order to visualize the people, places and events that figure in the articles he reads.

It was the ability to bring home to the reader often abstruse material that made J. D. Ratcliff the tremendously successful nonfiction writer he was. Graphically exemplified in his long series of *Reader's Digest* articles on the human body ("I Am Joe's Pancreas," liver, ear, foot, etc.) was Ratcliff's skill in involving the reader and dramatizing the factual details of his story.

Take "I Am Joe's Brain," for example (*Reader's Digest,* October 1973). The lead is dramatic: "Compared to me, the wonders of the universe pale into insignificance." Immediately following, Ratcliff tells us what the brain looks like: "a three-pound mushroom of gray and white tissue of gelatinous consistency." No need for diagrams or illustrations. From the start we have a mental picture that will stay with us as we read the paragraphs that follow. Into them are fitted a score or more statistical and other facts about Joe's brain, which is later likened to a telephone exchange and then to a "vast, unexplored continent." The skull, a "well-protected fortress" for the brain, encloses it; a blood-brain barrier serves as gatekeeper, letting some things in, denying entrance to others.

And so it goes. The figures are visual, the facts astounding. In conclusion: "My [the brain's] resources have barely been tapped." There is hope ahead for greater accomplishment. On this note of inspiration the article ends.

Factual though it is, the article is in effect and in structure a story. The same was true of each article in the series, published in book form as "I Am Joe's Body" and well worth study by anyone interested in writing for magazines.

In writing a magazine article, the author, while presenting almost any sort of material, will want to highlight its drama, whatever it may be, and show its impact on people in every way possible. Only so can the reader be made to empathize, to share what is going on.

Even in the straight factual piece the writer must remember to help readers by providing quick answers to the questions that will occur to them, perhaps unconsciously, as they read. (The margins of a promising article returned for revision are likely to be crammed with questions: How much? How many? Just when? Who is he? What does he look like? etc., etc.)

In working with new writers, the most common weakness I have found is the lack of specifics, the failure to pin down each and every generalization with a statement of fact or a concrete illustration. Anecdotal examples are often the most effective, although admittedly they do not always provide scientific proof. Direct quotes from authorities lend substance, but should not be overused. Language that evokes visual images can be immensely useful.

"An old, old gentleman we had known years ago turned up recently, tapping his way along the street," began a short piece in *The New Yorker.* A lead like this has concreteness, visual clarity. It evokes an image that engages attention immediately, which is precisely what the lead is supposed to accomplish.

Reader participation

Modern magazine writers often try to make the reader

feel he is participating in the experiences he reads about or believe, at any rate, that the writer has. The sharp lines once drawn between fiction and nonfiction have blurred somewhat as a result. Many a first-person piece today reads like a work of fiction, no matter how closely the author sticks to the facts in narrating what he has experienced or observed. "The Black Spot," subtitled "A personal encounter with cancer," was a true story, published in *The Atlantic Monthly,* of the writer's experience following his doctor's observation of a small melanoma on his back. Considerable suspense develops as the reader follows the detailed account of events and shares the writer's quite natural anxiety and his joy when the pathology report provides the hoped-for happy ending.

Instead of a straight factual report, an account of a new surgical technique may be written as if from the amphitheater where medical students (and the writer) watch every move of the surgeon's skillful hands as he operates on a patient whose name (usually fictitious), sex, and background may well be included in the text. An article about a well-known actress might recreate in the first few paragraphs the hustle and bustle behind scenes on opening night or the moment of quiet that sometimes precedes the roar of applause following a great performance.

In a basically informative article on cross-country skiing, published in *Ms.,* author Lynn Ferrin conveys so graphically her own joy in the increasingly popular sport that the reader can hardly resist joining in. The article starts off:

> One afternoon recently I was moving through the aspen trees at the edge of a meadow, feeling very fine about how the snow sounded under my skis and about the way my legs felt and

about how the late sun was rosy on the mountains. I passed near a group of other ski tourers and a man said to me, "Wow, you must have been cross-country skiing a long time."

"Oh," I answered, "five or six years. Why?"

"Because all your equipment is so tattered and grubby," he laughed.

I looked down at my well-scratched skis, my baggy patched knickers and my knuckles smiling through old green Army gloves.

Well yes, dammit, and that's one of the reasons I took up Nordic cross-country skiing in the first place. Because it doesn't matter how you look or how slow you go or how often you fall down. Because Nordic skiing is between you and the winter and no one else.

The text that follows includes all one needs to know about equipment, trails, cautions to observe, etc., all within the context of the writer's experience ("Years ago I paid $2 for a pair of used bamboo poles which still serve me well" ... "It's easy to economize with cross-country ski clothes. In thrift shops I've picked up nice soft old cashmere sweaters and wool shirts for less than $1 apiece.").

The article's ending leaves the reader with a feeling of vicarious experience, tempting him or her to try cross-country skiing, too:

The national parks are lovely beyond all imagining in winter. I've skied along the soaring rims of Yosemite Valley and Crater Lake and past the billowing steam vents of Lassen. I've glided through elk herds and watched the eagles play in the Grand Tetons, and seen Old Faithful erupt beneath the pale stars with just myself as witness. They say the north rim of the Grand Canyon is beginning to hear the swoosh of Nordic skis, and tourers are venturing into the high canyonlands of Utah and past the ancient Indian cave dwellings of New Mexico.

It will take me—and hopefully you—a lifetime of winters to know it all.

The same technique is widely used and obviously applicable in travel writing. The consistently readable travel section of *The New York Times* provides an example in "Robin Hood: He Was a Real Live Bloke," an article headed by a fanciful picture of the Major Oak of Sherwood Forest sheltering Robin Hood and members of his company. We join the writer and his family as they pursue the question of Robin Hood's reality, visiting the scenes in which, over the centuries, the story has variously been set, spending hours in the Nottingham Library and talking with residents of the area. Most of these experts on the subject are unanimous in their conviction that "he was a real live bloke," a conviction that, by the end of the article, the writer so obviously shares that the reader too comes away convinced.

Perhaps because of television with its undeniable, if sometimes painful, immediacy, the modern magazine article more often than not has this element of involvement. Magazine writers and editors are, after all, in direct competition with television, the medium that has threatened to steal their audiences but has so far notably failed to do so.

Impact and immediacy

Applicability also is important. The published article can have a direct impact on readers, encouraging them to use in their day-to-day lives knowledge they have gained from their reading. Many of today's more popular types of magazine articles—from straight how-to pieces that explain the rudiments of building a birdfeeder or pouring a cellar floor, to political articles that conclude by urging the reader to write his congressman—have the element of applicability. It's a rare issue of a women's magazine that fails to include articles on diet and sex, almost always offering advice for change—and, of course, improvement—in the reader's life and habits. Nor are these basic human concerns neglected in other magazines, from *Esquire* to *The Reader's Digest,* which also regularly publish articles dealing with these subjects.

Look for ways to make the articles you write have direct or potential application to your readers' lives, as Lynn Ferrin did in the final line (and elsewhere in the article too) of her piece on cross-country skiing. In planning and writing articles, watch for ways to give the material both applicability and immediacy. Best results will be achieved when your research extends beyond the library to encompass interviews, personal visits to places mentioned, observations that you yourself make.

In a *Redbook* article "On the Job: What It Takes for a Woman to Get Ahead" (January 1977), from which excerpts are reprinted below, Claire Safran takes the reader along with her on an informal survey of working conditions for women in factories, stores and business offices around the country. Although the investigation is on a limited scale, its findings have validity simply because we have participated in it along with the author, who names and briefly individualizes the various women whose opinions and attitudes she reports. For almost any woman who reads the article there is certain to be an element of involvement and applicability, be she a factory worker herself, a union member, a housebound mother of six, or a career woman on her way up. The article begins:

> It's bargaining day in Janesville, Wisconsin. At a union-management negotiating session the man who is head of the management team stares across the conference table at the factory worker who leads the union delegation—a dark-haired

woman not quite five feet two. He fingers his tie and confesses sheepishly, "It feels strange, talking economics with a woman." Janet King, mother of three, offers only a vague smile in reply, but months later, when she recalls the incident, she is 90 pounds of indignation. "Women work, don't they?" she fumes. "We bring home a pay check. We *know* what economics is all about."

In recent months I've been learning from women like Janet King about the importance of unions. Married to a factory hand who works nights "for the premium pay," she resents the public image of bluecollar workers. "Knock on wood," she says, "I don't know any Archie Bunkers, male or female."

Eight years ago Janet was among the first small group of women to be hired for the assembly line at Fox Corporation, manufacturers of minibikes and go-carts. She remembers the "crude" remarks of the men who felt things would never be the same now that women had arrived. They were right, but not in the way they expected.

"When we got here," Janet says, "there was no union, no insurance plan, nothing. We worked here for sixty days and then we got ourselves organized."

The women became the plant leaders, and wages and benefits went up for everyone. Janet began at $1.90 an hour, now earns $3.96 or about $8000 a year. If you ask Janet King, she'll tell you that a working woman's best friend is her labor union.

In the same way, an article about the Bronx Zoo or New York's famed Botanical Gardens might "take the reader along." Certainly such a piece would have to stem from a personal visit, although a trip to the library might well come first. Reading in advance about the sights to be seen, how the exhibits were collected, etc., will provide background for what you see, but the visit itself should supply the article's focus and dictate its shape. Will you concentrate on one section of New York's great zoo—the new aviary, the recently renovated Reptile House, or the African Plains collection? Or will you attempt to observe and record sensitively the various ways children react to the animals and draw conclusions from those observations? What you decide to do will, of course, be dictated in part by your own predilections. But circumstances will play a part, too. What, specifically, happens at the Zoo on the day of your visit? Is it bright and sunny or rainy and cold? Are the animals in their outdoor cages or cooped up unhappily inside? How do the place, the animals, the people affect you? Time out for notetaking will be time well spent. Quick snapshots of people and animals interacting will assist your memory and enrich the article. Very likely you will decide you need to spend another day or two in Bronx Park before you can coordinate your impressions and shape an article that incorporates them effectively. It would surely be helpful to chat with some of the keepers or seek out members of the administrative staff to whom you could put specific questions that have occurred to you. If you are lucky, you'll come on something newsworthy like the recent testing of birth control pills on the zoo's lioness, a development that might provide an entirely new focus for your article.

No matter how you decide to handle the material, immediacy can best be achieved by utilizing short-story techniques—setting the scene, helping the reader see and hear, perhaps even taste and smell, the environment in which the events described take place. Whatever the subject you are working on, through use of descriptive detail, carefully selected dialogue or direct quotation (your ears are as important as your eyes in recording usable detail) and the building up of the article to a climax or conclusion, you will be doing what you need to do to produce a magazine article that will appeal to today's reader.

~3~

How to Get Started in Article Writing

The new writer cannot expect to be given assignments at the very start, nor will he ordinarily have his articles accepted by the large, high-paying national magazines. But there are hundreds, if not thousands, of smaller publications that may prove to be good outlets for beginners' articles, if the material is carefully researched and written to the best of the writers' ability.

At whatever stage in life you tackle free-lance writing, there will be material available to you, and potential markets for the articles you write as well as experiences to draw upon. Women who are full-time homemakers need not postpone their writing until after the children start college or go off on their own. During their children's growing years, they may well have many perceptive, informative, or funny things to say not only about marriage, adolescence, or other domestic subjects, but about community or volunteer work and specialized topics in the fields of arts and letters—in other words, the whole range of subjects open to any writer, part- or full-time. A large proportion of women—married and unmarried, with or without children—work these days. Those who want to write must discipline themselves to make time for their writing, even if it is only an hour a day. And while some may look to their homes and children for their material, others will find subjects to match their interests, abilities, and work experiences, and discover they can produce salable material, no matter how short a time they allocate to writing—as long as they work at it regularly.

People who do wait until they retire before they pick up a pen may, if they have a writer's ear and eye, have accumulated (often without even knowing it) material for a number of pieces pertaining to their business or profession—or at least peripherally connected with their work experience. They may recollect dramatic confrontations from the business world—techniques of being interviewed for a job successfully; the effects of data processing on the people in the office; the pros and cons of an office Christmas party. Character-revealing incidents that took place on the golf course, or ski slopes, tennis courts, or office trips could provide material for human-interest articles of one type or another. A man I know pulled together in his first year of retirement his recollections of family sailing and made an entertaining and informative book, excerpts from which were published in *The Reader's Digest.*

If you are a retired man or woman with grown children, perhaps you have some thoughts on today's teen-ager, on fatherhood or motherhood and how attitudes toward children have changed—for better or worse—which might be excellent starting places for your writing. (Articles on these formerly "female" subjects are being published in increasing numbers under masculine by-lines, a reflection of the changing patterns in marriage, life styles, and the relations between the sexes.)

A man or woman, in the course of his or her work over a period of years, may have developed an expertise that can be shared with readers. Well-written, accurate, and clearly presented information on taxes, investments, banking (women as well as men now engage in all of these), for example, by well-qualified people appear in article form in many magazines and newspapers.

A young woman of my acquaintance, mother of a lively two-year-old boy, bemoaned the fact that, because of limited time, she was unable to get started on the "larger" writing projects she so much wanted to undertake. Somewhat apologetically, she showed me a scrapbook with clippings of a dozen or so provocative and entertaining full-length pieces she has sold to magazines that address themselves to young women. Starting with *Bride's Magazine* and *Modern Bride,* she had gone on to sell articles over a period of years to *Baby Talk* and *Baby Care,* then, most recently, to *Parents'.*

She had found all of the publications she has been dealing with so successfully pleasant to work with, eager for more of her articles, and prepared to pay good rates. She should probably stick with them for the time being. For now, her richest sources of material are her small son, her household, her reactions to motherhood, her family life, etc. She is writing precisely what she should be writing, for these are the things that matter to her most at this time in her life. Other projects will come later as the writer, her child, and her writing mature.

Informed discussion of the oil shortage from a former industry executive, advice on saving energy in the household from a retired electrical engineer, a discussion of effective sales techniques by an experienced salesman—these are kinds of articles that, carefully constructed and preferably

written in a lively style, will very likely sell to a service
magazine like *American Legion* or *Rotarian,* or as feature
articles for an area newspaper. Their specific content will, of
course, be drawn in part from the writer's own experience,
with anecdotes and remembered incidents comprising an
important element, at least from the point of view of
readability.

It took the tragic experience of bearing a baby afflicted
with Down's Syndrome to stimulate one writer I know to
become something of an authority on the problems of mental retardation and, in the process of her own education, to
write and sell articles on aspects of this subject to *Parents'*
and *The Reader's Digest,* as well as to professional journals.
Her personal concern lends force to articles presenting the
facts about retardation and urging increased attention to the
problem.

Writer enthusiasm

Funny or serious, topical or timeless, informative, philo-
sophical, sentimental, "significant," or whatever, the subject
should seem important to the writer. In order to persuade
the reader to spend time reading an article, there must be a
good reason for writing it. (A good laugh is, of course, as
valid a reason as any.) The editor's reaction to a piece that
fails to justify its own existence, as it were, is terse: "So
what?" he asks and tosses the manuscript on the reject
pile.

Over and over again I have observed that writers stand a
far better chance of bringing off successfully articles on
subjects they are themselves excited about. Indeed, the
article writer is by nature an enthusiast. In editorial offices
it is commonplace to encounter writers—and editors, too—

adopting ideas, products, innovations that have been described favorably in their articles. Be it solar heat or jogging, isometrics or the high-fiber diet, likely as not, the writer himself will be one of the first to try it out.

Enthusiasm isn't enough, of course. Hard work is required to produce a substantial article. Even a light art-of-living piece that grows right out of the writer's own experience will probably need a good deal of rewriting, rephrasing, discarding of lines and paragraphs that in the first version seemed eminently usable and even inspired. The simplest how-to article must be carefully researched and checked with experts in order to ensure complete accuracy. Writer and editor must take responsibility when they advise readers, and they must be prepared to stand behind the article if it is challenged.

Suppose you decide to develop a how-to article based on your own family's exciting success last year with its first vegetable garden. The whole experience was so satisfying that you are eager to let others know about it. As you talk with friends, you realize there are many who, like you, have never had a garden before but would like to have one now, although they feel unprepared for the project. Even as you write your query letter, you realize that your limited knowledge of the subject will require supplemental research. What you present in the query will be only the skeleton of the informative article you hope to write. But you have your own enthusiasm to work with. If the query letter not only assures the editor that the article will be informative but also promises an element of humor, of family camaraderie, an extra dimension in the treatment of a basically familiar subject, you may well win a nod of encouragement from the editor to whom the query is sent.

Make sure, by checking the *Readers' Guide to Periodical Literature* at your local library, that the subject has not been covered recently in the magazine you query. Briefly told, in anecdotal style, the story of your family's first vegetable-gardening experience could conceivably fit into the editorial schedule for a spring issue of one of the Sunday magazines. (*Boston Globe, Chicago Tribune, Philadelphia Bulletin,* and a number of other major newspapers publish such weekly supplements; *Family Magazine* is prepared each week to accompany Sunday editions of the three armed services publications, *Army, Navy* and *Air Force Times; UpCountry* is distributed once a month with the Sunday editions of several New England newspapers, etc.)

With emphasis on the family-togetherness angle, the piece might work out for *Parents' Magazine* or *Woman's Day.* To be effective, the article, wherever it is offered, will need anecdotes as well as lots of information and the breeziest, most colorful presentation you can put together.

Look, listen, and act

Subjects for articles lie all around. Writers learn to be alert to the careless remark, the provocative anecdote, the brief newspaper story or TV short that hints at the possibility of a moving or dramatic happening, a colorful personality of more than local significance or perhaps a success story that is shaping up in the writer's own home town. One writing friend of mine confided that her hairdressing appointments more than pay for themselves in the leads she picks up in that gossipy place. Most article writers are dedicated newspaper readers, making a point of buying local papers when they travel from place to place and watching the hometown paper for leads to local stories of potentially broader significance. The Sunday edition of *The New York Times* is available by mail, if not on the newsstands, everywhere in the United States and is a veritable gold mine of information and ideas. It also offers beginning writers excellent models of leads and general presentation of material. If you must go to the library every week to see the Sunday *Times,* do it. And read your local or regional paper daily or weekly, too.

The person who aspires to write and sell should learn to watch his own enthusiasms and work with them. Are you excited about a "cause"—the Nature Conservancy, your local animal shelter, the Save-the-Children Federation or Planned Parenthood? Your philanthropic interest may lead to material for an article. Regular mailings from the organizations espousing such causes are worth examining for their reports on newsworthy developments. Additional material will be readily available from organization headquarters.

Many writers break into print initially in the pages of their local newspapers. I know one (with two daughters in high school at the time) who got her start in magazine writing by landing an assignment to do a weekly column on education for her county paper. The assignment didn't come until she had submitted two or three carefully prepared sample columns on local school topics her daughters tipped her off to. Satisfied she could produce material readers of the paper would like to see, the editor signed her up for a year, offering little money, but giving her free rein in her choice of materials—as long as the columns pertained in some way to education, developments in the educational field, innovations, and experiments going on in the immediate area or in the state as a whole.

The column soon acquired a local reputation. People

began to phone with leads to likely stories. Two of the columns lent themselves to development as articles, and resulted in magazine sales. Those first sales led to others. After a year, the newspaper editor let her broaden the column's scope to include local celebrities, figures in the entertainment world, eccentrics and artists who lived in the area. The ever-widening circle of contacts led to more article subjects and now, ten years after that first column appeared, its author, a well-established free-lance writer, has trouble keeping up with the assignments that are offered her.

A bird-watcher down in Texas has a column in her county paper, in which she relates her ornithological experiences and encourages readers to send in their rare observations. After several years of this, the columnist had not only built up the bird-watcher population in central Texas to formidable proportions, but to her delight, she eventually sold a full-length article on birding to *The Reader's Digest,* thus introducing millions of readers to the joys of her favorite outdoor game.

Backyard treasures

If these examples seem to suggest the wisdom of starting close to home, that is precisely what they are intended to do. There is treasure in your own backyard, rich ore waiting to be mined in your own household and in the town where you live, if you will open your eyes and be alert to the possibilities that lie around you. Whenever you find yourself saying, "Someone should write an article about that," stop for a moment and consider if you might not be just the one to do the job. Are you having trouble with the department store where you have traded for twenty years? Now that their accounts have been computerized, you can't seem to convince them that months ago you paid the bill they keep dunning you for. Such exchanges of correspondence have sometimes provided the basis for lively articles with which readers, themselves confronted at every turn by the inscrutable computer, empathize wholeheartedly.

Your concern about the environment, if related to some specific issue, can be developed into article material. Conservation in all its aspects presents an almost infinitely varied choice of subject matter, ranging from at-home recycling programs to broad questions of national concern. A writer who focuses his or her efforts on conservation will find a number of magazines today that concentrate on conservation and environmental problems while most of the general interest magazines also regularly publish environmental material. Wildlife and outdoor publications like *Audubon, National Wildlife, Living Wilderness* and *Mountain Gazette* put special emphasis on the subject. Conservation is "in" these days, a concern of young and old alike. Political candidates are judged on the basis of the positions they take on controversial conservation questions. Whether we like it or not, we're all involved in such matters. Somewhere in every adult's experience or activities, there are bound to be connections with an ecology-related subject that could be developed in article form.

Popular topics

An interest in diet and nutrition and their importance to good health can provide an equally solid foundation for articles, especially if the writer can bring in incidents and illustrative anecdotes from his or her own experience, in addition to accurate information culled from authoritative

sources. A successful reducing program for an overweight
child, with information about the general problem of fat
children, how they get that way, and the importance of
altering their eating habits would be something that could
be sold to a variety of markets. There is, as we all know, a
tremendous interest these days in diet and health. There
seems no end to the articles that are published in this subject area, one that is of compelling concern to almost
everyone.

If the work you do for a living fascinates you, you may
want to share your excitement about it with others. A professional photographer, for example, undoubtedly has se-
crets to impart to amateur readers of *Popular Photography,*
or one of the other photo magazines. He might consider
developing a series of informed pieces on separate aspects of
the art of picture-taking for one of them. The editorial requirements of semi-technical publications are not stringent.
Professional qualifications and a hard-earned knowledge of
techniques, plus good illustrative examples, should easily
sell the idea for such a series.

As a successful salesperson, you may have discovered
some secret weapons that others could use to advantage. An
article describing these techniques, anecdotally illustrated,
could very likely be marketed to a business magazine, to
your own company's house organ or to an industry publication. Other possible markets for this sort of piece: *Rotarian,
Kiwanis* or *Lions' Magazine,* publications of the country's
three major service organizations, all markets for free-
lance material that will be of interest to the business and
professional people who read their magazines. (Of the three,
Kiwanis seems to be somewhat more family-oriented.)

There are many ways of developing job-related material.

Check the trade paper that serves the industry you are involved with or the house organ of the company you work for. Perhaps your particular job has the elements of a story in it. You may have been an eyewitness when something exciting happened that might be the basis of a piece for one of these publications. If you were on the scene with camera in hand, so much the better, for pictures are an important part of articles for this market, often being salable by themselves. An oil fire, an industrial accident, the opening of a new plant or the introduction of new equipment would be the sorts of subject that might lend themselves to development. Manufacturing companies like to publish articles that show their products in a favorable light. The major oil companies, with some of the biggest house organs in publication, provide markets worth remembering.

~ 4 ~

How-to and Fact Articles

There are almost as many ways of presenting a set of facts as there are writers who may attempt the task, for no two persons will express themselves in exactly the same way, even on the same subject. Many editors consider the how-to article the easiest and best for the beginner to tackle, and it continues to offer opportunities for experienced writers as well.

Writing has always had an educational aspect; the writer traditionally is a teacher. If a person has developed specialized skills, the world soon tracks him down and seeks to learn from him. And the writer, for his part, gains satisfaction from sharing the knowledge he has gained, often through many hours of patient work. There will be pleasure for him—and some monetary return, too—in guiding the footsteps of others as they strive to master the skill he knows so well.

There is a seemingly unlimited market for how-to articles, not only in specialized magazines but in more general ones as well. The "make-it, fix-it, grow-it magazine," as the editor of *How-To* describes his publication, suggests the range of subjects in the how-to category. But other magazines go beyond those areas, as, for example, in the *Woman's Day* piece, "How to Solve Problems Like an Expert," *Seventeen's* "How to Survive Strict Parents," and two articles in *Glamour* titled "17 Prime Places to Meet Men," and "How to Break with a Man Who Is Wrong for You." *Ms.* published advice on "How to Choose the Right Child Care Program." *Alaska Magazine* ran "How to Photograph the Brown Grizzly and Survive."

Clearly, the possibilities in the how-to article field are limited only by the writer's interest, experience, and specialized knowledge. It is always easier to write effectively and successfully when you have specific information and facts to convey. Your own favorite crafts, hobbies and avocations can provide material for salable articles—and writing them will almost certainly further your education too, for you will find yourself digging into background and fine points of your subject that you might not otherwise ever learn about. Although I have gardened for many years, it wasn't until I got an assignment to do an article on perennial gardens that I took the time to look up the history of flower gardening in the U.S., tracing it back to England and France, and even further, to China and Japan, where many of our most beautiful garden flowers originated. My own pleasure in my garden is permanently enhanced by this new knowledge.

, An article that persuasively describes the pleasure and benefit to be derived from some specialized craft—découpage, needlepoint, rug hooking—or conveys the delights of photography, oil painting or playing in a string quartet may sell to a magazine with a general readership, especially if the subject has never been covered in the magazine before. More limited treatment of some special aspect of it that you happen to know a lot about can be placed with the special-interest magazine that caters to fellow practitioners of the particular activity discussed.

Often the subject presented can be quite narrow in scope. How-to articles, usually brief, in *Organic Gardening* cover such specialized subjects as getting two crops of peas in Oklahoma, growing oak-leaf lettuce, and the return of the draft horse, with instructions on using this animal effectively and where to find the equipment needed to work with them.

Worth remembering too as a market for short how-to and other types of articles is *McCall's* "Right Now" section, a monthly potpourri of short reports (300 to 800 words) on such varied subjects as the new interest-bearing checking accounts, breast cancer, pressure massage and how to counter sex discrimination in housing (all covered in a single "Right Now" section).

In another version of the popular how-to approach, *Yankee* publishes a series on "Forgotten Arts," including articles on how to reclaim an old apple tree, on making paint from scratch (as our forefathers were obliged to do), on raising a small flock of chickens, and on maple-sugaring as it was done some forty years ago.

Fact articles about goings-on in the immediate area can often be sold to local daily or weekly newspapers or, in a metropolitan district, to the local city magazine. The story behind a local monument, the history of an 18th-century house that is a town landmark, the success of a small local business—these would be typical subjects. Some income and a lot of practical experience can be gained from writing for this sort of market, not to mention the encouragement the new writer derives from seeing his material—and his name— in print. Almost anything goes, so long as there is a local angle and the story promises to hold the attention of the paper's readers.

Hard-won knowledge on antique restoring, home painting, lawn building and maintenance, dog breeding and showing, or whatever, can be all—or almost all—you need to write a short piece that will sell easily to a magazine in the particular field involved. I say "almost all," because even this kind of article is likely to require a few trips to the library and some research to provide authority for the writer's unsupported statements. Successful examples will help make the article authentic, and illustrations and diagrams where appropriate will enhance its chance of selling.

An experienced do-it-yourself craftsman of my acquaintance has acquired quite a reputation in our neighborhood for his attractive handmade furniture and ingeniously fitted storage units. Eventually, his wife, tired of having the house cluttered up with people asking his advice on tools, materials, etc., suggested he write down some of the information in article form. With his wife's assistance this former non-writer produced a series of how-to pieces he had no difficulty selling for enough money to finance more projects. Fortunately for him, the wife in the team had had some training in commercial art and was able to do graphic illustrations to accompany his detailed instructions for putting together such diverse but useful objects as a blanket chest, a child's desk, floor-to-ceiling bookshelves, a garden toolhouse, and other household furnishings.

Eventually the wife, who was an enthusiastic and talented knitter and home sewer, decided that she too had knowledge she could share with others—for a profit. Her short, carefully illustrated pieces on knitting and home-sewing projects soon began to appear in needlework and crafts magazines.

Antique collecting presents a wealth of article subjects for the collector who takes the time to delve into the history and background of items in his own or friends' collections. The handsome Duncan Phyfe table that has come down through the family for several generations may have a story behind it that will entrance readers of *Antiques Journal, Antique Dealer* or, from a different angle, *Furniture and Furnishings.* Furniture refinishing, an art in itself, could be the focus of a variety of how-to articles. A piece in *Connecticut Magazine* described refinishing techniques in some detail, while reporting specifically on methods used by several of the state's better-known restorers.

Beekeeping was the focus of an interesting article in *Farmstead Magazine.* A short piece on a complicated subject like this cannot hope to cover it in depth. But the writer can present the fundamentals, at the same time sparking reader interest by conveying the author's excitement and enthusiasm about a hobby hitherto unknown or unfamiliar to most readers. Those who follow through will then seek additional information elsewhere—and indeed it is a function of the how-to article to guide the reader to further sources of information on the specialized subject it covers.

In another even more esoteric field, *Sky and Telescope,* a magazine for amateur astronomers, opened its pages to a how-to feature on homemade observatories, with brief reports on plans for and construction of home observatories and color pictures of the work in progress, all contributed by the magazine's readers.

If your spare time is spent largely in the garden, you may want to use this writer's avocation as a source of article material. In wintertime, if you share my passion for growing things, you putter over houseplants, start seedlings under lights, etc. Perhaps you have developed your own way of starting seeds or have had special success with a new strain of petunias that has proved easier to start than those you have grown in the past. You may have a special rig for staking your tomato plants or a new and easier method of building a compost pile.

Information about any of these discoveries of yours can be counted on to be of interest to readers of a garden magazine. *Organic Gardening,* for example, invites articles, to 2500 words, on organic agriculture, biological control of pests, compost and natural fertilizers. Full-length discussions and brief specific reports on all these subjects appear regularly in the magazine, which pays $50 to $200 for articles with photos or illustrations. Examination of a copy reveals that although much of the issue is staff-written, there are contributions as well from organic gardeners and farmers in all parts of the country. One reader reports on her ingenious use of her oven in germinating seeds for starting indoors, another describes her herb garden and offers hints for successful growing of herbs. The proper care of garden tools and methods of raising rabbits are subjects of other free-lance pieces in the same issue of the magazine. The material is largely in the how-to category and the editors apparently welcome articles based on almost any kind of gardening expertise that reflects a general acceptance of the organic method.

If your approach to gardening is not strictly organic, there are plenty of other markets for garden material, among them *Flower and Garden, The Family Food Garden, Family Circle, Horticulture* and *How-to.*

Pre-planning

Do a bit more thinking about the subject you have in

mind. Is this the right time of year to discuss tomato culture or composting—or rather, will it be the right time three or four months hence when an article you still have to research, write and submit to an editor might be scheduled for use in a magazine? If not, put that one aside for now and consider some of the other ideas that have occurred to you.

You might settle on a descriptive piece, with pictures you have fortunately been taking from time to time, on propagation by cuttings of houseplants and certain tender garden plants as well. Your methods do not require a greenhouse or any large outlay for materials. You have worked wonders, in fact, in what you call your "kitchen garden," actually, two ranks of shelves with long fluorescent "Gro-lamps" overhead. Yours happen to be situated in the ell at the back of your country-style kitchen, hence the name. They could as well be located in a warm dry cellar or even in a well-ventilated attic space.

First-person accounts of methods used successfully in building or making something, illustrated with photos and diagrams if possible, often make marketable articles. Typical is a piece in *American Home* on how to build a backyard tennis court, with detailed information on costs, materials, and zoning laws (which would vary for different areas, but readers would *learn* that such ordinances have to be looked into). Similarly, an illustrated article, "Dry Stone Walls: Building Them to Last," by Julian Fish, appeared in *Early American Life* (April 1976). Here is how it began:

> Some years ago I purchased a run-down, circa 1790 salt-box
> on fifteen acres of land. During the course of putting both
> house and grounds in shape, I wanted stone walls in certain
> areas in addition to those already on the property. Since I could
> not find anyone either to build them for me or to tell me how

to build them, I started a lengthy process of trial and error to discover the method, or *a* method, of building a substantial dry stone wall. The effort was successful.

A lasting dry stone wall must meet the following requirements: Not fall down by being pushed, leaned against or walked upon (running is not advised); not be affected by frost action; not be disturbed by ground vibration from falling trees, lightning or road traffic.

When building such a wall, there is one attitude to keep constantly in mind: *Every stone and rock is usable,* as the stones are stacked, not fitted. The pioneers had no time to be selective; their objective was to get the stones out of the field and to build a wall that would stand.

With this introduction, the author proceeded to outline the four steps involved in construction of a dry stone wall and to suggest possible sources of stone, adding a few cautions and a summary of the benefits (almost no maintenance, attractive appearance, etc.). The conclusion:

Easy-does-it to build a wall that will enhance your property and last, untouched, for generations.

How-to articles usually require research, even when the writer has first-hand knowledge of his subject to start with. But if competently done, they are almost sure to sell, either to an appropriate specialized publication, to a general-interest magazine or to one of the larger house organs, which regularly solicit material of this sort. By zeroing in on just one aspect of a broader field, it is often possible to develop a fresh view that will be easily marketable. Your way of making a concrete walk or a stone wall, if it works (as it did in these examples) is a legitimate focus for an article, as is your particular technique for freezing fresh vegetables, making bread or persuading your dog not to bark while tied outdoors.

Fact articles

There are, obviously, many other kinds of factual articles
in addition to the strictly instructional how-to piece. Informative discussions of practically every subject under the sun
are published every year in U.S. magazines. Science and
invention, history, travel and education are major fields
covered, but there are many others—astronomy, zoology,
botany, space exploration, rocks and minerals, mountain
climbing. The list could go on and on, with the title of a
specialized magazine noted under virtually every heading.
But informative, newsworthy articles in all these fields are
often sold to general-interest publications too. The key
word here is newsworthy. To get special-interest material
into a general magazine there has to be an element of timeli-
ness in the piece, a new discovery, a breakthrough of some
sort that justifies bringing up the subject now. In this re-
spect the Bicentennial was a blessing to writers with a taste
for historical subjects. During the period of its celebration
the anniversary itself made many subjects timely that would
not otherwise win space in any but the most specialized
publications. But every year there are certain nationally
celebrated anniversaries that make pertinent historical
material timely in the month in which the date falls.

Historical subjects when colorfully presented and made
to relate somehow to current events are usually marketable.
Yankee regularly publishes articles that reflect aspects of
New England's past. *Mankind* devotes itself to "popular
history," while *American Heritage* covers the broad sweep
of our nation's past.

Don't overlook the regionals, which now cover every part
of the United States, including Alaska (three magazines are
published regularly in the 49th State). A number of cities

have their own publications, as do New York State's West-
chester County and Connecticut's Fairfield County. Such
regionals as *Philadelphia, Charlotte, Arizona Highways, West
Virginia, New Mexico, Vermont Life* or *Connecticut,* to
name just a few, use material about the men and women
who shaped the history of their regions. Commemoration of
battles and stories of life in early days often appear in these
publications.

Generally, the regionals look for articles on local personalities and enterprises, local problems and political issues,
newsworthy innovations, profiles of famous people living in
their areas. But a certain amount of space in a magazine like
Charlotte, for example, is devoted to general-interest material with a local slant. An article entitled "How to Stay
Healthy While Keeping Fit" did so this way:

> Current research suggests that where you live may have some-
> thing to do with your physical well-being.
> In Charlotte the disease and mortality data indicate that we
> are in pretty good shape for the shape we are in. But the avail-
> ability of physical conditioning facilities is sometimes a
> problem.

Later in the article the author recommends a treadmill
EKG ("stress test") at Charlotte's Memorial Hospital and
mentions the cost of the service, going on to describe his
own experience on the treadmill. But the article, with these
few exceptions, could have appeared in any magazine across
the country, for the subject is of general interest and the
advice it contains potentially helpful to readers wherever
they may live.

On the other hand, the same magazine ran an article on
"Soya Plus," describing a new imitation milk, available so

far only to persons living in or near Charlotte. Most of the rest of the magazine is strictly local in interest. The balance is probably fairly representative of regional publications, with the exception of those, like *Arizona Highways,* that confine themselves strictly to photographic and descriptive coverage of the state.

~ 5 ~

Inspirational Articles: Self-Help, Art of Living and Personal Experience

Inspirational articles tend to lean more heavily on the author's own experience than do the factual pieces discussed in the previous chapter (although, as we have seen, how-to pieces too sometimes grow out of the writer's own hobbies and special interests). Inspirational articles comprise a large category of magazine nonfiction for which there is always a ready demand.

Self-help

Inspiration, in its original sense, involves divine influence or revelation. Religious experience of this sort, convincingly narrated, can be counted on to find an audience. But in a broader sense, inspiration, Webster tells us, is "the action or power of moving the intellect or emotions." Thus articles can "inspire" readers to improve their lives in many different ways and in this sense self-help articles of all kinds are inspirational, whether or not they involve religious experience. There is a large and steady demand for the kind of piece that encourages readers to take up new activities—exercise, yoga, transcendental meditation, transactional analysis, new languages, belly dancing, group therapy—in order to acquire greater self-knowledge, a better figure, a happier life. Or, on a more down-to-earth level, there are self-help articles dealing with household management, adjustment to divorce, parent-child relations, making your co-workers like you and a host of other common life situations.

Self-help articles are to be found regularly in major publications and in the small or less well-known denominational magazines as well. An article in *Ms.*, for example, titled "Making Time: a Housewife's Log," explained how the author came to keep a diary (sample sections were quoted, providing an entertaining change of pace) and what she learned from it about improving her work habits and her relationship with her family.

"Children Make the Greatest Teachers" was the theme of an appealing article in *Woman's Day* by a mother who drew her subject matter from several years of nursery school teaching and the sayings and doings of her own small children. What author Leslie Kenton learned from them is summarized in the following paragraph from the article:

> Like most adults, I've learned to live for goals. I have lost the great joy of the seeking itself by relegating that part of my life to the "unpleasant duty of working for what I want." Yet many of life's pleasures are to be found as much in the seeking as in the finding. Young children have helped me see this—although I am a long way from putting it into practice in everything I do.

Art of living

While similar in some respects to the straight how-to

piece, like all inspirational articles, the self-help article draws on the author's personal experience for its material. Clearly allied to it and also inspirational in a general sense are what editors call "art of living" articles. These focus on a central theme, illustrating it with anecdotes and remembered details drawn from the writer's own experience and observation (much as a minister might build a sermon around a theme—honesty, greed, brotherhood, lust—using Biblical quotes and anecdotes to drive home his points). The art of living piece always points the way to a better life, suggesting that readers apply its message to the solution of their personal problems.

Marjorie Holmes, who has had phenomenal success with art of living and self help material presented in both article and book form, attributes her success, with disarming modesty, to the fact that she was "hamstrung by an innate fear of legwork." More important, the ideas Mrs. Holmes wanted to express "came not from outside sources, but from my own reflections, observations and convictions. The trick was in simply making them applicable to everybody else," she wrote in the introduction to her book, *Writing the Creative Article* (The Writer, Inc.).

This sort of article, persuasively written, gives readers the feeling that they too can make progress toward improving themselves and the quality of their lives. Close observation of and sensitivity to the problems of others and attention to the means used to handle them are excellent bases for inspirational pieces. Use of fiction techniques, anecdotal leads and the buildup of "characters," using simulated dialogue to bring incidents and experiences to life for the reader—all these are important in all kinds of inspirational writing, which, you will remember, must move not only the intellect but the emotions.

The art of living article, more abstract than the straight self-help piece, often describes in an inspiring and dramatic way how the author's experience (or that of someone in his family or among his friends) of living under stress or through tragedy and coming out triumphant has made him a better, stronger person. Senator Frank Church concluded his account of his near-fatal encounter with cancer almost thirty years ago ("I Was Told I Had Only Six Months To Live," *Good Housekeeping,* January 1976), as follows:

> I decided never to be afraid of reaching too high or too far too soon. Failing in an ambitious effort could not possibly be as defeating as facing terminal cancer. That's why I ran for the United States Senate in 1956 at an age some people considered absurdly young—I was 32—and against odds which some people considered absurdly high—I was pitted against some of Idaho's best established political figures. I took the chance and won. Suddenly I was embarked on a political career which some say might lead to the Presidency. (Though, as I write this now, in the fall of 1975, I have not yet decided to run for that office.) It has been an enormously satisfying career, one which I've found to be a hefty stimulation to mind and spirit. But if it had not been for the insight on life and death which my struggle with cancer provided, I might have waited and waited and waited. And never found the nerve to try.

Like the short story, the art of living article frequently requires some characterization; it demands too a degree of skill in compressing anecdotal material while retaining essentials. Dialogue may be used, for quotes often get across to the reader better than straight description the kind of person involved in the story. At the same time, the dialogue develops the article's central theme or builds up to its conclusion.

Sometimes the art of living article offers down-to-earth advice on an everyday situation. *Woman's Day,* for instance, ran "Who's Boss in Your Marriage?" full of specific tips on maintaining a marital balance. Art of living themes may turn up in the course of the daily routine, at the office or at home. Depending on its content and setting, this sort of piece can be placed in a general magazine or in a quite specialized one, if the action or examples and anecdotal material have pertinence for the particular audience of that magazine. A piece involving a doctor who learned something significant about human nature in the course of his practice might well appeal to one of the several magazines published especially for doctors.

Because so many magazines publish art of living articles, this sort of material is highly salable, even by beginning writers. *The Reader's Digest, Guideposts,* the in-flight magazines put out by almost every airline for its passengers, and Sunday magazines, as well as the straight religious or denominational magazines, are markets for art of living articles.

Art of living articles that present persuasively certain broad religious or ethical truths or demonstrate dramatically the working of faith or the efficacy of prayer may often be found in such publications as *Christian Century, Christian Herald,* and similar magazines. "Wheelchair Missioners," by Rosemary Edwards, the account of a family stricken by muscular dystrophy and of how their faith supported them and gave them courage in the face of tragedy (published in *Maryknoll Magazine*), carried a direct religious message to the magazine's Catholic readers.

Even nature and outdoors magazines, as well as various magazines for children, sometimes publish art of living arti-

cles. The women's magazines welcome them too, if they
focus on family situations, the solution to marital conflicts,
problems of working mothers, widowhood, loneliness, and
similar subjects, and show how the author or central character coped successfully with the problem. One of the men's
magazines might react favorably to a lively account of a
boy's struggle to succeed in the sport his father excelled in
(though he disliked sports), or to a piece focusing on a
dramatic incident in Little League baseball or high school
football that illustrates some significant aspect of human
relations. Many sports articles are in fact basically art of
living pieces that emphasize the nobler side of human nature. The national preoccupation with sports is in a sense
justified in magazine articles that stress this heroic behavior and focus on how racial discrimination is lessened on the
playing field. If prejudice can be erased on the tennis court
and the golf course, then it can be dissipated in the population as a whole, such articles implicitly suggest.

Although they may require little or no research, the
apparent simplicity of art of living pieces can be decep-
tive. To write a successful art of living article, the writer
must bring to the material observations and reflections on
human nature that will be significant for readers to whom
the experience, whatever it is, may be unfamiliar, perhaps
even strange and bizarre. The theme, therefore, must have
an element of universality, and must be appealingly
presented.

Personal experience articles

Many magazines look for personal experience articles,
recognizing that there is at least one story in every one of
us, writer and non-writer alike. *The Reader's Digest* pays

top prices for what it calls "Drama in Real Life," and has also published since 1955 a very successful series of colorful features under the running head, "First Person Award Stories."

Almost without exception, *Digest* First Person Award winners are writers whose work has never been published before. Their dramatic accounts, each one derived from its author's life experience, make exciting and satisfying reading. Search your own past (or present) for comparable material—exciting events that may have been almost lost in your memory but could be reconstructed now in narrative form. Adolph Sutro did just that when he wrote "Lift-Off from San Francisco Bay," (*Reader's Digest*), a hair-raising account of the day back in 1913 when the author, now in his eighties, and two friends set three world records in the homemade flying machine he had made in his mother's backyard. Other *Digest* First Person writers have recounted dramatic war experiences, surviving a typhoon, living through an earthquake, being caught in a forest fire, etc. The list is long, the experiences narrated almost infinitely varied, but all, in one way or another, dramatic. And in every case it is the graphically recalled experience of the writer that makes the story.

Followed up with on-the-spot research, a brief news item may open up an exciting account of human drama, a brush with death, perhaps, or the disclosure of unsung personal heroism, courageous behavior by an individual coping with serious illness or injury. Be on the watch for news items that might be leads, especially (to be practical) reports emanating from places within easy reach of where you live. Real-life adventures of all sorts, spotted in the course of careful newspaper coverage, can provide material for articles that will sell readily to the men's magazines or, if done in depth, may qualify as "Drama in Real Life" in *The Reader's Digest.*

Actually, most magazines welcome a genuinely exciting adventure story. "Shipwreck," about the sinking of a small boat by a whale and the survival of the young couple who were on it, appeared in *Good Housekeeping.* The piece was very likely prompted by a brief news item spotted by writer Elizabeth Keiffer and followed up with a request for an interview.

Personal accounts of psychic experiences, if convincingly related, can find a variety of markets, large and small. *The Reader's Digest* pays high rates for this kind of piece, but there are many other general and specialized markets for such material. Among the latter are *ESP, New Realities,* and other publications in the field of extrasensory perception and parapsychology. And the *Digest* is by no means the only general magazine that might be interested, if you have a believable ghost story to tell. There is a perennial appeal to the well-told tale of psychic experience that lingers like a question in the reader's mind.

There are articles in you and your experiences, and around you in other people and what happens to them. One such article combined both elements with outstanding success. In his piece in *Yankee,* titled "The Word Man," Bill Conklin wrote of his family's move from Manhattan to a small town in Vermont. The crisply anecdotal account of the Conklins' gradual adjustment to the new environment, the puzzlement of the villagers and the eventual rapprochement between them makes for an entertaining and quietly moving story that only this author could tell because it happened to him.

Sometimes an article simply has to be written. The very act of setting down on paper the details of a painful experience may be a form of therapy. So it was with my daughter, wife of an Air Force officer, whose youngest boy, a husky three-year-old, was bitten by a rattlesnake while on a walk with his mother near their home on the Air Force reservation outside Colorado Springs several years ago. Despite immediate and heroic efforts to save his life, little Mike, whose small body could not handle the rigorous treatment required to counteract the venom, slipped away finally after two weeks in a coma so deep the doctors told his parents there would have been severe brain damage had he survived.

Writing of her tragic experience helped the bereaved mother find a sort of meaning in what had happened. In helping others to meet the loss of those dear to them, she managed also to help herself.

Writing things down imposes a sort of rationality on them, makes them make sense, as it were. "We have met death and it has not conquered us," my daughter concluded on a note of triumph that brings tears to my eyes now as I reread her courageous little article, published in one of the Catholic magazines a few months after my grandson's death.

Sex in nonfiction writing

In another direction entirely, the spate of sex articles— and books, too—is a striking phenomenon of our times. These days sex seems to be a major preoccupation of many people, or perhaps it is simply that now they are talking freely about it. At any rate, articles dealing with aspects of the sexual revolution, your own experiences in this area, changing attitudes toward sex education (in schools, by parents, etc.), should find a ready market. A wide range of magazines on the stands cover this subject, from the out-and-out sex-oriented publications to the more general magazines like *Good Housekeeping, Ms., Ladies' Home Journal, McCall's, Redbook, Cosmopolitan, Mademoiselle, Harper's Bazaar,* and countless more. A sampling of titles from these magazines will convey the scope of what is regularly found in them on the subject of sex: "When Women Find Sex Disappointing," "Advice about Unconsummated Marriages," "Giving and Getting Sexual Pleasure," "Rediscover Sex with Your Husband," "Coping with Unfaithfulness," "The Erotic Diet," "How's Your Sex Life: Better, Worse, I Forget."

Sooner or later, all of us encounter aspects of sex in our lives or are troubled by problems arising from sex relations or our own sexuality. Helpful, sensible articles on subjects like these are in wide demand, especially if they have authority behind them (a book, for example, or quotes from a doctor or marriage counselor or therapist). They should be written sensitively, with good taste, to establish a common ground with a maximum number of readers who in all probability share these all too human concerns.

This broad field of subject matter lends itself to development in different ways and from many points of view. Increasingly frank discussions of sex appear in today's magazines. There now seems literally nothing that cannot be discussed in print with the greatest openness. Such articles are to be found every month not only in the new women's magazines like *Ms., New Woman* and *Working Woman,* in *Esquire* and *Playboy* and others of their ilk, but even in the pages of such traditionally family-oriented publications as *Redbook, Ladies' Home Journal* and *Good Housekeeping.*

By no means all sex articles are written by "experts."

Experiences in marriage—and outside it—experience with abortion, sterilization, impotence, rape, teen-age sex—have all been covered in magazine articles and can be used again by the individual writer to convey sometimes painfully acquired knowledge. Homosexuality, once taboo, is today freely discussed, and homosexual experiences described in as much detail as the heterosexual situations that were once the only acceptable bases for discussions of sex. "Sexy" titles have always been used to sell magazines at newsstands. Nowadays, there is every likelihood that the article itself will actually live up to the promise of the title.

The new freedom of discussion of once-taboo subjects makes for new opportunities for writers. Both men and women who are interested in developing material for the magazines should be on the watch for new insights and perceptions they can use in articles that will interest readers and help them cope with the often troubling problems of sex relations.

~ 6 ~

The Humorous Article

There is always a market for the really funny article or anecdote. Readers love the writer who can make them laugh and so, for that matter, do editors. Often, there is great artistry in the truly humorous piece.

Be on the alert for amusing situations, picturesque turns of speech, humorous mistakes that you may make, or comical episodes that typify your relationships with other members of your family. These can be the material you need to work with *if* you are the sort of person who tends to see humor in life's drama and to laugh heartily, not only at the ludicrous happenings that befall others, but also at your own misfortunes and frustrations.

Subjects for humor

Frustration is an important element in humor and many successful pieces of humorous writing reveal the writer's (or the main character's) inability to handle problems familiar to everyone. Instead of losing your temper next time the screwdriver disappears or your teen-age son wrecks the lawnmower or your spouse invites your least favorite neighbors for dinner, stand back a moment and try to see the humor in the situation. Do you often lose your tools and, after a great hubbub, find them in what you sheepishly admit is the place where *you* put them? Perhaps there is the making of a brief humorous piece in that characteristic of yours, for it is one with which many readers can identify.

Funny incidents in your life or in the lives of others you know or hear about can be all you need to start you off. A visit to a new dentist who fills your mouth with cotton wads and then fires questions at you; getting a ticket for speeding when you're on your way to work and already late; your son's advice on how to dress in the latest style; a court appearance to defend your delinquent dog, an habitual wanderer—every day brings humorous subjects, if you are on the lookout for them. Incongruity between what is expected and what happens is a traditional source of humor.

Even serious subjects can produce humorous side effects: a new life pattern that finds the man running the house while his wife works or goes to school; the woman who answers an "equal employment" job ad, then wonders how she came to be spending her days in the hot sun directing traffic around a road construction job. Such experiences are becoming more common as sex roles change; there is a sympathetic audience for articles pointing out the humor in what may not, to the participants, seem like terribly funny situations.

While humorous pieces usually grow out of real-life situations, the writer need not feel bound to stick strictly to facts. An element of exaggeration is common to this kind of writing, even when the narration is in the first person. Walt Schmidt framed his piece, "The Man Who Watched 1,500

Late Late Movies" (*The Saturday Evening Post,* May 1975),
in interview form. Parts of it follow:

> REPORTER: How is it you are the all-time champion watcher
> of late-late movies?
> MAN: Well, before TV I chased girls. But when I finally married
> one, I found out she was a talker. In self-defense I turned to
> watching movies while she talked.
> REPORTER: How could you enjoy television over your wife's
> talking?
> MAN: It was easy. I just stared at the television set and pre-
> tended I was listening to her.
> REPORTER: Has watching TV movies changed you in any
> way?
> MAN: I don't think so. But my wife complains I smoke cigars
> like Groucho Marx, talk like Charlie Ruggles and walk like
> Charlie Chaplin.
> REPORTER: Has listening to TV movies affected the harmony
> of your married life?
> MAN: My wife has grown used to communicating on family
> problems while the commercials are on. Sometimes during a
> movie I can see her shaking her fist and yelling something at
> me, but I can snow her out by increasing the volume on
> remote control.
> REPORTER: Has she ever threatened to leave?
> MAN: Lately, every time I open the refrigerator door I see a
> note telling me she is through. That she's going to split the
> scene.
> REPORTER: How long has this been going on?
> MAN: For the past month. Come to think of it, I haven't seen
> her for a month.
> REPORTER: Maybe it's the same note. Maybe you'd better
> look around the rest of the house?
> MAN: I'll do that between movies tonight. But right now you'll
> have to excuse me ... *Bonnie and Clyde* is about to start. I
> just have time to run out to the kitchen for some potato
> chips and beer while the tube is warming up.

Fantasy, if it has a basic point and keeps within its self-imposed restrictions, sometimes works well. An example: "Put Your Head in Your Hand and Let Your Mind Roll By," in *New Woman,* the story of Wellington Whim, a successful manufacturer of Whimsicals, and his girl friend Wilma, who finally stood up to him.

In "Therapy for Dogs," reprinted below in condensed form from *UpCountry,* author Newton F. Tolman must surely stray a little beyond the strict confines of fact, but he writes with such deadpan seriousness the reader is tempted to believe.

After my wife retired from the kennel and bird-dog business, she found life intolerably lonely and dull with only two or three dogs around. Almost without any conscious plan, she started to take "just one more dog" when some old friend, off to Europe or wherever, couldn't face leaving her pet in an ordinary kennel.

Living in the intimacy of our house with us and our own dogs, most of these visitors displayed emotional problems of various sorts. This led my wife to discover a new and exciting field—a sort of encounter group employing various therapies. In our daily workshops we deal purely and simply with problems of the inner dog—in short, problems of personality and emotion. For example, a dog may not adjust well, peer-wise, because of an unusually large tail; a dog may feel unable to sleep any place except in my armchair; a dog from a suburban background may reveal an obsessive impulse to relate to porcupines, and so on.

At our workshops, the dogs are all directed to lie down on the floor in a circle. For a time they are encouraged merely to hold each other's paws. Next, each dog is told to look directly into the eyes of the dog lying nearest for several minutes. Finally, each dog is allowed to smell the dog of its own choosing.

Almost without exception, owners report that dogs who have spent only a few weeks in our encounter groups return home with personalities so changed as to be quite unrecognizable. We have applied for a government grant. It is our hope that in the future our plan will be expanded to embrace similar centers throughout the nation.

Note: The Center is booked to capacity for the coming year. No referrals can be accepted.

National Review published Aloise B. Heath's piece about Christmas in her family of ten children. It was her bright idea to adopt a practice of the famous Trapp family in the hope of instilling in her offspring some of the real spirit of Chrismas. The experiment didn't work quite as she expected and a number of funny things happened in the process, most of them revelatory of the Heath family's life and relationships. The idea was for each child to pick the name of another child for whom, during the pre-Christmas season, he or she would do a good turn every day. After a good deal of argument about who would be whose Christkindl (the plan is alleged to work beautifully in the Trapp family), Mrs. Heath finally did the drawing. Even then, there were problems. The children finally worked out their own solution, reported below by their mother:

> Every Sunday now, they each buy seven penny lollipops and every night they slip a lollipop under their Christkindl's pillow. Well, I *know* that doesn't sound so terribly spiritual, but it's better than what they used to do. What they used to do was steal each other's lollipops.

The only free-lance material solicited by *National Review,* a conservative political journal, is "short prose satire to 900 words." Although her piece was somewhat longer than that, the editors evidently bent the rules to admit Mrs. Heath's delightful article.

The work of those humorous writers you find most *simpatico*—the ones who can make you laugh aloud—will provide models of excellence. Did you laugh out loud as you wrote your piece? Did it seem to improve as you worked over it? Humorous writing is a serious business. In all likelihood, the more effortless it looks, the more work went into it. (The serious part is the rewriting; the laughs come the first time round.)

Almost any editor will agree that there is never an over-supply of usable humorous material. While other kinds of articles may pile up in inventory, funny pieces are used immediately. More often than not, the editor finds himself without an extra one on hand—or, at any rate, without one he thinks is funny enough to use.

The editorial requirements of house organs listed in the *Gebbie House Magazine Directory* include frequent references to humor (and to cartoons, which seem to be an almost universal need in these company magazines). Even if most of your writing is of a different sort, don't miss the opportunity to try a humorous article when some situation in your life strikes you as containing the basis for one: your daughter's wedding, a son's first visit home after a couple of months as a freshman in college, your struggles with the local plumber, a New England character who flatly refuses to let you spend money on new fixtures when the old will do as well (never mind that your wife has her heart set on changing the bathroom decor). This is the sort of simple close-to-home situation that can be built into a piece that makes readers chuckle sympathetically. You'll never know until you try whether you too can write articles that will make people laugh!

Politics, public life, the PTA, planning and running a

meeting, the behavior of people in public life, friends who take themselves too seriously, habits of family members—these can be the nuclei for humorous pieces, if you are willing to laugh at yourself, perhaps by showing how some eccentricity of yours was responsible for a marital or household crisis. Readers will readily identify with this kind of humorous approach to a human foible and be subtly comforted by the knowledge that others share their own peculiarities or bad habits.

One writer concocted an amusing short piece for *Modern Maturity* out of her own absent-mindedness, which leads her to put things in strange places, forget names and dates, and, she says, shampoo her hair with hand lotion after watering the geraniums with bleach. "Over the Cuckoo's Nest," by Tricia Hurst, concludes appropriately:

> If this article doesn't appear, it will probably be because it's lining a cookie sheet and the editor is sitting there wondering what I expect him to do with a piece of aluminum foil. If he has any insight at all, he'll make a funny pointed hat out of it and send it back. I'll put it on immediately—that is, if I can find my head.

Writing humor is not easy, although, when well done, it appears to be. While humorous articles are likely to be short, for laughs cannot be drawn out too long and knowing when to stop is important, it takes a lot of work and polishing to cut the extraneous and shape each paragraph to produce the most laughs, making sure to wring every bit of humor out of the situation or idea while sticking close to it. No matter what the subject, the humorous article must focus directly on it. Every word and line used should serve in some way to build up to the laugh.

There is another aspect of humorous writing that is perhaps even more important to article writers than the development of straight humorous pieces. Magazines, remember, are *not* required reading. Most people read them primarily for entertainment, although they expect to learn from them too, of course. But this sort of learning is expected to be pleasurable (readers want the pill to come with a sugar coating!). If the writer's style is slow-moving and stodgy, most readers won't finish the article. Indeed, if you don't take hold of the reader at the beginning, you have probably lost him forever. A heavy-handed lead may do just that. Try using a light touch instead—on the lead and, if appropriate, throughout the article. Subjects that don't benefit from a bright, lively presentation are few and far between and not likely to be topics you will tackle in your early efforts at magazine article writing.

Here is Blair Sabol's lead for an article titled "A Yankee Pilgrim in the Old South," published in *The New York Times Magazine:*

> It's called the rise of the New South and it has something to do with serving grits instead of pasta at plush soirees; printing "yawl come" on gold-engraved party invitations; square-dancing instead of doing the hustle at your neighborhood disco; actually marrying your live-in boy- or girl-friend or returning home to your estranged spouse for good this time; acquiring a complete set of Gregg Allman or Dolly Parton records; wearing denims and a cardigan sweater to board meetings. Now combine all of that with our President's flannel shirts and a "Gone with the Wind" telecast which took the ratings by storm, and you've got to admit that the South not only shall rise but *has* risen and *keeps on* rising again and again.

Ms. Sabol's report on Natchez and its traditional Confederate Pageant continues in the same vein, succeeding in conveying very effectively, always with a light touch, the flavor of the Old South as it is recreated every spring in the Mississippi city. At the end of her stay she was persuaded to don a hoop skirt and stand in a receiving line with her hostesses. Her lively account of her experiences concludes:

> My Southern fling ended somewhat disastrously in the Adams' guest bathroom. As I wrestled for my life with my hoop skirts, I tore one of the petticoats and drowned one of the hem's silken roses in the commode. It was then that I realized I would never make it as a moonlight magnolia. This Scarlett O'Hara business is hard work.

The famous "*New Yorker* style" is basically the result of the editors' insistence that writers handle their material, no matter how serious it may be, deftly and with a light touch. While some of the leavening is undoubtedly the work of the magazine's copy editors, however it is accomplished, the result is a sort of brightness that illumines the sometimes over-long profile or report on a new technological development, ensuring its readability.

A bright lead can help set the tone of an article, as in *The New York Times Magazine* piece quoted above. Frances Minturn Howard opened her short informative article on Boston's swan boat concession, published in *Yankee,* as follows:

> Let others look for the shy hepatica, the elusive snowdrop, the hardy crocus as the first sign of spring. To a true Bostonian, it isn't spring till the swan boats appear on the little lake in the Public Garden. As they have for 100 years.

It was probably the light touch, applied to an informative

factual piece on dog-obedience classes that sold Anne Barry's article on the subject to *Cosmopolitan,* not the likeliest market for the piece. Too long to quote in full, the article contained all the necessary information on dog-training classes. But, as the following excerpts will show, there was an added dimension:

> "Help is at hand," I told my dog. "You and I are going to develop a meaningful relationship based on my giving the orders and your being practically perfect."

The two head for the first class, "a three-ring circus with an all-dog cast." The instructor gives commands that the dogs ignore, but gradually, as the class progresses, "The light dawns slowly."

> The dogs aren't the students—we *owners* are. Beatrice, now wrapping her leash in a figure eight around my ankles, does not have a learning problem. I have a *teaching* problem.

This, of course, is the crux of the matter and the article's main point. It is conveyed so lightly and easily that we hardly know we are being instructed. The lessons culminate in a mock dog show in which Beatrice performs splendidly while her owner, the narrator, gets stage fright, forgets how to do the turns and walks off in the wrong direction. Even so, they win a blue ribbon for the dog's performance.

In your reading, watch for examples of the light touch, felicitously used. Note that writers who succeed with it are often outstandingly successful in marketing their articles. Note, too, that the light touch can be applied to the most serious of subjects, as it was, at least in the lead, in *The*

Atlantic Monthly article, "Science That Frightens Scientists," by William Bennett and Joel Gurin. Here is how the two writers opened their discussion of recombinant DNA:

> The rules of the game have not changed for upwards of three billion years: every living creature is dealt a genetic hand, the best stay in for another round. Five years ago in California a few biochemists learned how to stack the deck. They contrived a method for mixing, at will, genes from any two organisms on the planet. Genes cause a creature to be like its relatives and unlike anything else. They say, in a universal chemical language, "Wings, not feet; brown feathers, not blue; quack, not warble"; or "orange fruit, not yellow; pungent, not bland; round, not elongated."

Examples could be multiplied. Perhaps those quoted above are enough to convey the message, underlined in red: Don't be afraid to use a light touch in handling even the most difficult or serious subjects. Strive to make your prose readable, colorful and lively in order to keep readers with you.

~ 7 ~

Interviews, Profiles, and Personality Features

Personality pieces for newspapers provide an excellent way for the beginning article writer to break into print. Newspapers lean heavily on the interview as the basis for feature articles, but magazine pieces are often essentially interviews, too, sometimes even published in question-and-answer form. A local "success story" may lead to a feature piece based on an interview with the man or woman whose achievement has received news coverage. It is difficult to arrange interviews with famous personages, unless they happen to come from your area and you have some access to them, perhaps when they come home for a visit or on a promotion circuit in connection with a new film, play or book.

The personality piece not only gives a new writer valuable experience, but it can be done in spare time, for publication in the local press or a regional magazine, or even in the in-house publication of the place where the writer works. This kind of profile may fit the needs of the specialized magazines like *The Elks, Rotarian* or *The Lion* that go to members of fraternal organizations, especially if the subject happens to be a member of the group that sponsors the magazine. Even some of the religious and denominational newspapers or magazines occasionally use short articles of this sort. A colorful local priest who has espoused an unusual cause or served the church for a period in some exotic foreign country might be an appealing focus for an article in one of the Catholic publications, for example.

Who, what and where

It is a good idea to watch your local paper for brief reports on newly elected or appointed officials. New members of the Board of Education, of selection committees for judges, officers of wine-tasting societies or gourmet gatherings, the new head librarian at your public library—these are individuals whose accomplishments or activities may be of interest to a large number of people in the area, making them good subjects for personality articles, and such people are usually willing (sometimes eager) to grant an interview.

A few experiences of this sort on the local level should give the writer the confidence needed to request an interview with the national celebrity scheduled to speak at some local function or vacationing nearby, perhaps building a house in the writer's own town. A brief news item plus a little research to determine background facts can be the springboard for an article developed on the basis of the subsequent interview.

Doctors and dentists in the town where you live are in touch with their national professional organizations and sometimes serve as officers in them. By keeping in touch with local medical personnel, you can learn of the latest advances in their particular specialties, advances that may provide material for articles in the local papers or for submission to magazines.

Right in your locality there is almost certainly a wide range of people whose particular expertise or special contacts are of potential use to you as leads to or material for salable articles. Apply yourself to the task of finding them and arranging to talk with them. The effort will certainly pay off.

While it is probably best to think at the outset in terms of local outlets for such material, often business magazines or trade journals are interested too in articles relating to the work and "extra-curricular" achievements of local men and women who have invented, promoted or achieved something worthy of special notice, either in their work or in the community.

A magazine interview is usually done in greater depth than a newspaper feature. But with a new angle, even a familiar personality becomes newsworthy again. The famous actress who has recently retired, or who comes to visit her high school to help them stage a play or to her college to accept an honorary degree might make an article for a local or even a national publication, as long as the material can be documented, either by an interview or published sources.

The various Sunday supplements or so-called Sunday magazines are good markets for the personality-interview-profile article that may center on a local celebrity or highlight the accomplishments of a hitherto undiscovered talented person living in the area. Local dailies or weeklies that serve a group of towns in one area often run one or more personality features in every issue. The publication of a book by a local author may prompt an interview or profile for the local papers. An artist may be opening a show or teaching a class that has caused some excitement and engendered a new local interest in art. A talented local

musician may give a concert or play in the town orchestra
or with a group of local musicians and get a start; he or she
may win an audition as a result. Interviews with such personalities give area newspaper readers a new insight into the
local celebrity's life and work, suggesting how he or she lives
and what motivates his or her creative expression.

Setting up and conducting an interview

In the preparation of all but the slightest of pieces, an
interview or two will probably be necessary—not only for
the "interview-profile" feature, but for most kinds of
articles. If you are lucky, you may find someone right in
your hometown who can add a new dimension to the
material you have gleaned from published sources. Usually a
note or phone call asking for an appointment will open the
door to you.

Explain what you are writing, how you plan to approach
your subject, and what you hope the person interviewed can
contribute to your article. Have at least one or two opening
questions ready, and then be prepared to listen as he or she
talks about what will probably be a favorite topic. Express
your own interest and enthusiasm by asking intelligent questions. Take notes of anything you think you may be able to
use in your article. Later, if necessary, you can send your
interviewee a copy of the material you plan to quote, or
you may read it back on the telephone to check its accuracy. Take special note of the dramatic incident or newsworthy statistic.

You may need to give the person or persons interviewed
credit in your article manuscript. The anecdotal material
you glean from interviews will almost certainly be usable,
even if some of the stodgy statistics and dull facts you laboriously record end up on the discard pile.

Writers who do a lot of interviewing invariably emphasize the importance of listening for anecdotes and for quotable statements and picturesque phrases that convey the individual flavor of the subject's speech. Many writers use a tape recorder for interviews, but it is wise to get permission first. Some people feel nervous or inhibited with a tape recorder on the desk between them and the interviewer.

For other writers, it is more satisfactory to dispense with the recorder and take quick notes instead. Notes should be sufficiently detailed to jog your memory later when you sit down at the typewriter to write the article. Either way, prepared questions are helpful to get the subject started. Most people become voluble when questioned about their work. Advance preparation is essential. "If he's written a book, read it," one successful writer of interview articles told me. "If he's designed a new kind of windmill, bone up on windmills and windpower. If he's painted a picture, study it. Then you will be ready with the right question when the interview begins to flag."

Writers can't afford to be timid. One feature article writer I know—she happens to be a 50-year-old grandmother—went up in a sailplane with a former German test pilot in order to do a piece on soaring. To get material for an article on the Outward Bound program, this same intrepid lady scaled a rock face with ropes and pulleys and went kayaking in Pelham Bay. A piece about snakes took her into a rattler's den with the local herpetologist, who answered the questions she fired at him while he noted the size of the rattlers and condition of the skin on the big snake that lay coiled and watchful in a dark corner of the dank cave.

Writers who make successful use of the interview are usually individuals who genuinely like people and instinctively relate to them. For them interviewing is fun because they are really interested in what makes people tick. They find it easy to establish rapport. A thank you letter after the interview is courteous, and if the article is published, the writer should make sure that a copy of the magazine with the piece is sent to the person interviewed. Any questionable quotes should be checked for accuracy before publication.

~ 8 ~

Specialized Magazines

Although the specialized magazines, geared to every imaginable taste and designed to appeal to the interests of particular groups of people, limit their subject matter accordingly, their editors are seeking the best, most readable material they can find that will fit into their particular format. Competition between magazines aimed at the same audiences is keen.

Just as followers of the various competitive sports have their own magazines, so do the thousands of poeple who collect—stamps, antiques, gems, dolls, coins—and one or more magazines focus on each area of collecting. And because as animal lovers we rival the British, such magazines as *Cats, Cat Fancy, Dog World, Dogs, Horseman, Horse, Of Course* and *Horsemen's Journal,* among many others, cater to that large audience. *National Humane Review* and *Animal Kingdom* are other markets for animal stories. If, then, you are a "cat person," *Cat Fancy* and *Cats* would be likely markets for you. Both publish articles about felines, their care, grooming, and activities, as well as accounts of unusual experiences involving cats. Consider, too, the possibility of offering your cat (or other pet) articles to your weekly town or county newspaper, a promising outlet for material in this category. A sale might lead to an invitation to submit other pieces or even to encouragement of a regular weekly column centering on your own and your neighbors' experiences with pets.

Denominational magazines

Not to be overlooked by the beginning writer are the scores of denominational publications, many of which publish some general-interest material in every issue, offering a market to outside contributors without regard to church affiliation. Catholics, Protestants and Jews—with subdivisions of these into their various ideological factions—all have publications of their own. The sectarian magazines are major markets for inspirational and strictly religious material and for informational articles of certain kinds, too. Their editorial content is surprisingly varied. One issue of *Christian Herald,* for example, contained, in addition to two articles on meditation, a piece by Senator Mark Hatfield protesting the CIA's use of foreign missions and missionaries; a story with pictures about the surviving nineteenth-century frontier churches; an art of living piece on "The Art of Leaving"; and a semi-humorous defense, by a youth worker, of his tendency to lie abed later than his fellow workers.

Guideposts, a non-denominational inspirational magazine, looks for simple anecdotal articles in the first person on applying faith to everyday life, a definition of perhaps broader scope than appears at first glance. It pays $100 to $200 for articles of 750 to 1,500 words, less for shorter pieces. *Christian Family, Christian Life, A.D., Christianity and Crisis* and *Decision* (a Billy Graham publication), *Com-*

mentary (Jewish), *Catholic World* and *Commonweal, Christianity Today* and many others solicit material reflecting aspects of religious faith and the applications of religion in modern life, as well as general-interest material with only peripherally religious emphasis. Most of them pay for what they publish, although payments quite naturally aren't as high as in big-circulation publications that carry a greater volume of more lucrative advertising. Still, there is the satisfaction of seeing the article in print and the very real value to you of being able to cite some credits when, later, you send a query to the editor of a large-circulation magazine.

Travel

Travel magazines comprise another large market for a variety of material. A number of the 40-odd magazines regularly publishing travel material are backed by individual airlines and distributed in flight. National Airlines, Braniff, PanAm, North Central, Pacific Southwest, Eastern and TWA all have magazines of their own that lay heavy stress on travel material. The last mentioned, incidentally, offers up to $600 for 1,000- to 2,500-word travel articles with color transparencies, but also invites humorous pieces and material on sports, business, etc., that will interest the international readership of the airline's *TWA Ambassador.* A query is suggested.

Travel, Travel and Leisure and *Holiday* have general distribution and pay good rates for travel pieces of all sorts. *National Geographic,* in a category of its own, invites "first-person narratives on geography" and welcomes good color transparencies submitted with them. (The *Geographic,* paying $1,500 to $3,500 and up, on acceptance, is probably not a promising market for the beginner unless he or she has something really spectacular in the way of pictures and text to offer.) The travel section of the Sunday *New York Times* frequently publishes material by free-lance writers.

Obviously there are many markets for travel material. Next time you plan a trip, be it a family outing to a nearby state park or a long-planned vacation in Europe, dust off your camera, buy a supply of film and make sure to take it and a notebook along on your excursion. If you travel by car, consider *Ford Times* or the Allstate Motor Club's *Discovery* as possible markets for articles. Both pay well; both seek material related to motoring. A plane trip will open up another group of markets—the airlines-sponsored publications. Try the elegantly produced *Gourmet* and *Bon Appetit*, if dining in fine restaurants is part of your travel experience.

Although the above by no means exhausts the list, it is enough to suggest the breadth of the market for material on travel, a market that seems certain to grow along with the ever-growing enthusiasm for travel itself.

"Closed circulation" publications

Among markets you might overlook are the dozens—perhaps hundreds—of "closed-circulation" magazines. These are published for the members of certain organizations or professions and circulated free to those who pay their annual dues. Some, although never seen on newsstands, have surprisingly large circulations and pay good rates for editorial material. Some closed-circulation magazines welcome queries and free-lance submissions and regularly list their editorial needs in the various market guides. *Modern Maturity* and *Dynamic Maturity*, published for the 3,000,000 members of the American Association of Retired Persons, often publish free-lance articles, paying for them at rates comparable to those offered by openly circulated magazines. In the field of education, such magazines as *Change, American Education, Learning* and *Phi Delta Kappan* invite queries from free-lance writers. Both *National Geographic*, distributed to members of the National Geographic Society, and *Smithsonian,* which is sent to the membership of the Smithsonian Institution, publish the occasional free-lance article.

House organs and trade papers emanating from industry provide still another potential market for the beginner, although here again one must be selective. The *Gebbie House Magazine Directory,* carefully used, can be helpful to free-lance writers, for the larger house magazines, some of them with circulations (to employees and stockholders) of several hundred thousand, do solicit articles and pay well for acceptable material. In practically every case, the listing in *Gebbie* urges the would-be contributor to limit his offerings to product-related material and to send only articles and photos (house organs are good markets for photos and for cartoons) that have a direct bearing on the company's product.

Trade papers, distinguished from house organs by the fact that they carry advertising, aim to reach a more varied audience of opinion-makers, not necessarily having any connection with the company or companies (frequently they are sponsored by industry associations) that back the publication. But they, too, want relevant material. *Petroleum Today,* for example, serves the oil industry. It is published by the American Petroleum Institute, and every article in *Petroleum Today* relates significantly in some way to the industry it serves.

Listings for many trade and business magazines that are interested in free-lance material, such as *The Apothecary, Amusement Business, Aquarium Industry, Broadcast Engineering, Boating Industry, Big Farmer* and many others, appear in *The Writer* and *The Writer's Handbook,* and there are more to be found in *The Gebbie House Magazine Directory.* There are writers who have found it worthwhile to concentrate on producing material for the trade publications.

For young, old, and in-betweens

There are magazines published for the young, for the mature, and for the vast audiences in between, readers from twenty to forty years old. *Modern Maturity* and *Dynamic Maturity* understandably cater to the retired and over-50 group, as does *Retirement Living,* and there are others, like *Yankee,* that publish material for the mature audience. Writers who want to reach this market should keep this in mind, but not make the mistake of thinking that the interests and activities of this group are limited: the modern oldster is involved in everything from politics to pets, and the articles published reflect this wide range.

There are many magazines for young people, from beginning readers to young adults. There are such standbys as *Jack and Jill, Children's Digest, Highlights,* and *Humpty Dumpty,* and a large number of magazines for children put out by religious and denominational groups. More recently, the number of magazines for children of various ages has been increased by the addition of *Cricket, National Geographic World* (for 8-to-12-year-olds), and *Ebony, Jr.* (for 6-to-12-year-olds).

Articles on common problems of childhood and the

teen-age years are included in young people's magazines, as are pieces on young sports personalities, movie and television performers. One writer has established a continuing connection with *Young Miss,* selling them articles regularly, under their general heading of "Youth Beat." A recent one was on "Getting Along with Your Teachers," a problem most teen-agers have to cope with from time to time.

Don't think that children and teen-agers are easy audiences to write for: they are often extremely knowledgeable about their specialties and hobbies, and quick to spot any errors of fact in articles about them. Also, they don't feel any obligation (as they may with texts) to finish what they start in magazines they read for pleasure and entertainment. The writing must be lively and fast-paced, light in tone when appropriate, and never patronizing, in order to hold the attention of youthful readers.

Organizations and associations

Colorful and attractive magazines go to the members of various organizations, associations, and ethnic and religious groups—The Elks, Rotarians, Lions International, Masons and Knights of Columbus are only a few—and many of these associations have several magazines, each catering to a different age group or serving a different function for the organization. Writers will also find that such nonprofit groups as The National Humane Society publish their own magazines—*National Humane Review* is theirs; the Wilderness Society puts out a beautiful quarterly called *Living Wilderness* and invites queries. *Scouting* serves leaders of both Boy and Girl Scout troops. Experience as a Scout leader might provide the basis of an article that would be helpful to an audience coping with the same problems you did when, as a Cub Scout leader, you took on a group of 8- to 10-year-olds. Or, in the course of your Scouting experience, you may have been a more or less unwilling participant in a moment of high drama—a near drowning, an exciting mountain-climbing incident or a long search for a lost child. Such a happening, carefully reconstructed, can make the sort of "drama in real life" piece that is welcomed not only in the smaller outdoor magazines, but in large publications like *Good Housekeeping* or *The Reader's Digest.*

New magazines, new directions

There is a wide range of new specialized magazines (some 400 magazines start each year). In some the specialization is in the audience served, rather than in the editorial focus; others are technical and highly specialized in their content. *Identity* and *I-Am,* both new, both directed to Italian-Americans, will presumably undertake to represent the interests and reflect the lives of the country's largest ethnic group, but within that limitation both plan a broad coverage of the American scene, offering a potential free-lance market for writers who have access to material relevant to the Italian-American scene.

Quest/77 (the year will change annually) "dedicates itself to revealing human greatness, and to doing so with wit, sensitivity, and sophistication." *Working Woman,* an attractive new entry in the field of women's magazines, is billed as "as stylish as *Vogue,* as sensible as *Good Housekeeping,* as revealing as *People,* as businesslike as *Fortune,* as timely as *Time* itself."

There are a number of "people magazines," including the

successful Time-Life publication of that name (*People*), largely composed of material about personalities in the news, in the entertainment world, and the like. Two others seem to be aimed at the same market—*US* and *You* (for the young sophisticated audience). Though these are not generally open to free-lance material, some will look at queries on personality pieces.

Never since our country's beginnings have magazines flourished in greater variety and colorful richness than they do today. A glance at any well-stocked newsstand reveals a dizzying assortment of attractive covers.

The techniques that are used and useful in writing articles for the major national magazines are required also in preparing material for specialized and small publications. The lively lead, the use of fiction techniques, engaging the senses, maintaining variety of style and pace to avoid monotony—all of these considerations are equally essential to the craft of article writing for any age group or any kind of publication. Specific aspects of a subject may prompt you to direct the article to the readership of a specialized publication, but the way the material is presented must reflect knowledge, research, and skill acquired through practice.

~ 9 ~

Leads and Endings

The article or nonfiction story at its best is constructed like a short story, with a beginning, a middle and an end. The beginning is called the "lead." These first sentences or paragraphs can make the difference between an article that sells and one that is rejected. For it is the opening, if carefully thought out, written with authority and effectively worded, that takes readers by the hand and leads them, willing followers, straight into the article that follows.

Anything that serves right at the outset to catch the attention and win the confidence—first of the editor and then of the reader—is money in the writer's pocket. Among weaknesses found in article manuscripts returned to their writers for revision or rejection, the lead presents the most frequent problem. Writers would do well to give careful attention to their introductory sentences or paragraphs.

There are many kinds of leads. It is up to the writer to use the style and type of opening that best suits the material and the publication toward which the article may be aimed. If it is a humorous piece, a lively anecdote, complete with dialogue and characters (made up, if necessary) may be the appropriate way to begin. As a lead for a serious article, you may still use an anecdote, but one that is less humorous in content and is clearly related to the subject matter.

Action leads

In a personal experience article, an action lead might seem best fitted to take the reader into the dramatic story that follows, but such leads are effective at the start of other kinds of pieces also.

The following action leads all appeared in published articles, as noted:

> The cold and blowing snow were so intense that our eyelids froze open. About halfway up we were climbing simultaneously but roped in order to speed the ascent when suddenly Denny's snow step broke. He screamed "Falling!" as he wrenched onto his back and plummeted out of sight into the swirling, white abyss. After an eternity, the rope ran out and stretched taut to my seat harness. Incredibly, I was not ripped loose. I yelled down to Denny and he shouted that he was all right. He had fallen down 120 feet of rock bands and snow steps onto a steep snow slope, where he was hanging upside down.
>
> "Living on Mount Logan,"
> by P. S. Marshall,
> *Alaska Magazine* (March 1976)

> A bullet cracked past the car window.
> *He's shooting at us!* I thought. I floored the accelerator, the car leaped forward.
> Some friends and I had been lifting tires from a junkyard when the owner pulled up. Now in my rearview mirror I could see the bright flashes of his gun. I twisted the wheel and we shot into an alley. We screeched to a stop and all four of us exploded from the car.
>
> "I Want to Be Like You,"
> by Larry Wagner,
> *Guideposts* (January 1976)

When I opened the fortune cookie my husband Mark brought to my hospital room, I had to laugh. I read the words, "Many a girl is anxious to have her loose ends tied up," and realized that someone in that Chinese bakery knows about today's fastest growing method of birth control—laparoscopic tubal sterilization.

> "My Belly-Button Surgery,"
> by Sally Wendkos Olds,
> *Family Health* (April 1977)

An amoeba committed suicide as I watched one day. At first it swam about in the drop of pond water beneath the cover slide, gliding to the edge, withdrawing, a fragile morsel of probing protoplasm. Then it burst, sudden victim of osmotic processes designed to protect it against external stress. In that alien environment, it simply overdosed on fluid intake and ruptured.

> "Mystery Diseases,"
> by Sarah Harriman,
> *Connecticut* (March 1977)

Susie Brown, age 25, has a list of priorities for her day, and by midafternoon most of them are checked off. The house is sparkling, the baby has had an airing in the park, dinner is ready to be popped into the oven. *Check.* She dials her husband's office number. "John darling," she whispers into the phone. "I really crave your body." *Double check.*

She scans the newspapers, tears out an ad for a lingerie sale. Spotting a story about a football player who's been traded to another team, she practices how to say his name (John has this thing about football). At five o'clock she stands before her clothes closet planning what to wear when John gets home.

> "Can the Total Woman 'Magic' Work for You?"
> by Claire Safran,
> *Redbook* (February 1976)

Saturday morning, November 15. One A.M. The air is cold and clear in town, colder and clearer on the East River. One of the entrance ramps to the Brooklyn Bridge is also cold and clear—clear except for a car and a young runner; hunter and prey. The young runner is staggering on slippered feet as he propels himself up the ramp, heading for Brooklyn, trying desperately to lose his pursuer. He is wearing blood, sweat and pajama bottoms. He looks just like Dustin Hoffman.

He is Dustin Hoffman.

"How to Make a Movie in New York,"
by Ellen Stern,
New York Magazine (December 29, 1975)

Seventeen-year-old Jeff was pacing the floor outside the industrial arts room, but he didn't enter the class with the others when the bell rang. When his teacher came by and invited him inside, Jeff said he couldn't "think" because he had some problems. Lightly the teacher told Jeff to come to class as soon as he solved his problems. As the teacher started to leave Jeff asked him to wait a minute.

"I really can't think," said Jeff. "These problems . . . they take nine months to solve."

"Oh, *those* kinds of problems," said Jeff's teacher.

"Teenage Decision: Whether to Go on the Pill,"
by Peggy Fisher,
Maine Times (March 4, 1977)

The action lead, if successful, makes it hard for the reader to put the article down. It will draw an editor on, too, which is what you have to do to sell the manuscript. Something has to happen right there at the start, an incident or dramatic occurrence that needs explanation—to be found only in the article that follows.

A different sort of beginning may do the trick, too. Here's one, spun right out of its author's imagination, that would surely make any (female) editor read on:

Here is the fantasy: I am sitting in my office doing my job (which is being a journalist and which I adore; they have to drag

me out screaming to take my vacation), when the phone rings.
It is a Mr. Sulzberger of the *New York Times,* and he would like
to know if I am free for lunch next Thursday. Unfortunately,
on Thursday I am lunching with a Mrs. Schiff of the *New York
Post* and Friday is no good either, because a Mrs. Graham from
Washington is flying up to have lunch with me.

"Going by the Book: A Look at Career Guides for Women,"
by Carol Rinzler,
Working Woman (December 1976)

Anecdotal leads

If you are fortunate, somewhere in the course of your
research you will come on an anecdote, a little-known fact
or a colorful quote that is just what is needed to get your
piece off to a good start. Be on the alert for lead material as
you work your way through your published sources and as
you interview individuals who may have lively and revealing
recollections to contribute.

As the lead for an informative article on investment in
Cosmopolitan, financial expert Eliot Janeway told the following story:

Back in the Gilded Age, around 1917, a certain Morton
Plant, proud possessor of one of New York's stately mansions,
went over to Cartier's, at the time considered the city's most
prestigious purveyor of jewels. "I hear you're cramped for
space," Plant told Louis Cartier, the firm's founder. "Why don't
you expand and buy my house?" His price: one and a half
million dollars. Cartier refused the offer, but suggested instead
that Plant accept a magnificent pearl necklace valued, he said, at
the same amount. The deal was closed and Cartier's moved into
its present site on Fifth Avenue, now worth many times the
original price.

Meanwhile, as Janeway points out, once the Japanese
developed cultured pearls, the value of the necklace
dropped sharply. Which, says the author, simply shows that

pearls and diamonds are definitely not a girl's best friend. The famed economist then went on to present, for *Cosmo's* presumably female readership, his ten rules for wise investment.

When you get down to the business of writing, spare no pains in developing the lead. Remember that the opening of the article *is* the lead into what follows and must be pertinent to it while in one way or another setting the tone or suggesting the direction the article will take—as in the following, from an article (from *American Artist*) on illustrator Frank Frazetta:

> It is rare that an illustrator reaches a point in his career where he creates work and the publisher searches for an appropriate text to fit it, and should he not find one to fit, uses it anyway! Frank Frazetta has reached this point, and the publishers who purchase first printing rights to his work are delighted to get it, gleefully admitting that a Frazetta cover guarantees success for them.

Expository leads

Another kind of lead that can be equally effective in the right place is the explanatory or expository lead. In contrast with the action or anecdotal lead, explanatory leads are more straightforward, sometimes even summarizing the article that follows. This does not mean that these leads must or should be dull. As the following examples reveal, explanatory leads may contain fictional elements and utilize various devices to catch reader attention:

> There was no question about the diagnosis. Edith Brownlee had tuberculosis. But even in a little farm town of 5000 in southern Illinois at the turn of the century, there was still a chance. A chance that Edith Brownlee might live to see her four young daughters grow up.

It would take time though. Long agonizing months in bed, good medical care and money. Money that Tom Brownlee didn't have just now. At twenty-eight, Tom had a little hardware store that was just getting started and he was having a hard enough time feeding his family, let alone being able to afford a long illness and doctor bills.

Dr. Finney knew that too, but Edith had four girls to raise. He knew he might never get a dime for his services, but he'd known Tom since he was a boy, and he'd brought Edith into the world.

> "One Vote for Small Town Living,"
> by Paul William Barada,
> *The Country Gentleman* (Winter 75/76)

Looking at the world through the eyes of a child can transform humdrum reality into a magical land of the unexpected. "Cigars are fattening," my eight-year-old son Jesse announced one day. "I know because all the men who smoke them are fat."

Children have incredible wit and freshness. Everything seems new to them. The most trivial event can bring a child the kind of pleasure we adults spend a lot of money searching for. But that's not all. Sometimes, in subtle ways, they teach us truths that we might otherwise overlook.

> "Children Make the Greatest Teachers,"
> by Leslie Kenton,
> *Woman's Day* (April 1976)

When I die, perhaps I'll get a chance to chat with the master of campers. He'll probably ask me to recall the highlights of my short stay on Planet Earth.

"Right at the top, Sir," I'll reply, "was living and camping in Coconino County, Arizona."

For almost three decades I have motored and tramped across this unique chunk of America and I have come to know it intimately and to love it.

> "Coconino County,"
> by James Tallon,
> *Camping Journal* (May 1977)

Marge met Betty for the first time last summer at a friend's boating party and hated her on sight. The negative reaction

Marge felt was swift, irrational and so ferocious she couldn't wait until the lovely summer weekend had finished. "A little later," Marge told me, "I found out Betty had once been Jack's mistress and had tried to break up our marriage."

Like the rest of us, Marge has five senses: hearing, sight, smell, taste and touch, but no one of these senses could account for the animosity she felt for Betty. Like the rest of us, Marge also has instincts: she smiles when she feels friendly, flinches if menaced, and flees or fights if in danger. But neither could these instincts altogether account for the dismay and disgust she felt in Betty's presence. Marge also has something *beyond* senses or instincts; sometimes, she *knows* . . . she just knows. And this faculty, knowing without knowing how we know, is the one we call intuition.

> "Intuition—You've Got It, Use It!"
> by Irma Kurtz,
> *Cosmopolitan* (February 1976)

Expository leads tend to be longer and more detailed than other kinds of article openings. Often they state the substance of the piece in a few sentences that the article itself subsequently elaborates. Garry Wills began the article he entitled "Hurrah for Politicians" (*Harper's Magazine*) with this all-encompassing paragraph:

Politicians have many virtues that ignorant people take for vices. The principal ones are: (1) compromise of principle; (2) egotism; (3) mediocrity. In other men these may be vices, but for the politician they are needed skills—so much so that if a politician is not born with them, he must learn them; and if he does not learn them, he will either fail himself or do harm to others, as Eugene McCarthy did.

The opening of a far-ranging article on Toronto ("Canada's Dowager Learns to Swing," by E. A. Starbird), published in the August 1975 *National Geographic,* combined action and exposition:

The portly New Yorker picked up his briefcase and prepared to deplane in Toronto. "Would you believe it: This is my fifth trip up here in a month. 'You own the company,' my wife tells me, 'so send someone else for a change.' I tried it—with my sales manager. A real good man. He never came back."

Such is the danger of doing business in today's Toronto, home of rapid riches and solid fortune, of vibrant pace and quiet challenge. For this once-sedate city has become a rival to reckon with: worldly, wealthy, personable and relatively problem-free.

Sometimes a strictly visual picture provides the best starting point. A long and richly illustrated article on Tanzania ("Tanzania Marches to Its Own Drum," by Peter T. White, *National Geographic,* April 1975) began this way:

Under the equatorial sun in East Africa, in the Dodoma region of the United Republic of Tanzania, a little girl with a big gourd on her head walks into a dry riverbed. With her hands she digs a hole in the soft sand, arm-deep. She waits until enough muddy water has seeped into the hole to fill her gourd; then she walks back a quarter of a mile to a row of grape seedlings to pour a bit of water on each.

The picture is unforgettable. Its pathos establishes the courage and capacity for hard work of the Tanzanians in the face of seemingly insurmountable problems, a focal theme of the article that follows.

A lead shouldn't be complicated. John Philip Baumgardt began a useful article in *The New York Times* garden section straightforwardly:

Every good garden and every good gardener ought to have a cold frame. These small enclosures make all the difference.

The article went on to tell how and why.

Short quotes or a few lines of real or imagined dialogue at the start can do a lot to relieve the plodding monotony of a long informational article or to make a point effectively. Dialogue and quotes provide lively beginnings for two articles on marital problems:

> My friend Tania was raging against the fates and her newly exed-husband. "There was nothing wrong," she was saying. "We were blissful. And then one day he just up and said he'd fallen in love with someone else and he wanted out."
>
> It sounded horrendous. Paul was a villain. I comforted Tania and tried to say soothing things, but I never for a moment believed her. I had known their marriage was coming apart. How come she hadn't known? But when I mentioned this, she wailed, "What do you mean you knew? We never fought. We agreed about everything. I helped him in his work and he helped me in mine. In bed we were tigers, as hot for each other the day he left as the day we met."
>
> "Then how come you always stood at opposite ends of the room when you were at parties?" I asked.
>
> "Breaking Up—What It's All About,"
> by Linda Wolfe,
> *Cosmopolitan* (February 1976)

> "Larry says he loves and respects me intellectually, but my body leaves him cold," says 23-year-old Sandra, a pink-cheeked, blue-eyed blonde, five-feet-six, who weighed 128 curvy, becoming pounds. "Unless I lose at least ten more pounds, he says he can't force himself to feel sexually interested in me. At the rare meals we eat together—Larry holds two sales jobs and works incredibly long hours—he watches every bite I swallow, counting the calories."
>
> "Can This Marriage Be Saved?"
> by Dorothy Cameron Disney,
> *Ladies' Home Journal* (January 1976)

That opening packs a lot into a few quoted lines, along
with graphic identification of the speaker. Often, at or near
the start of an article, the writer will sketch his subject in a
few words of description that give the reader a visual image
to retain as he absorbs the text that follows:

> In the freshly mown fields, Western Pacific's red caboose
> Number 694 stands rusty and flaking in the moist warmth of
> the northern California summer. Smoke curls out of a stovepipe
> poking up from its roof. The only sounds are the busy noise of
> bees from a nearby hive, the territorial screech of redwing black-
> birds.
>
> A blond woman emerges from the back of the caboose where
> she has just finished cooking over a woodburning stove. Her hair
> is gathered off her pretty, sun-freckled face into an old green
> cloth; a thin coating of dust clings to her handmade skirt.
> Trailed by a barefoot four-year-old with hair that is almost
> white in the sun, she spreads some dinner scraps on a compost
> pile and then walks over to shade herself for a moment in a
> stand of locust trees.
>
>

"To Be Young, Rich and Happy in America,"
by Peter Collier and David Horowitz,
Esquire (February 1976)
>

> At first glance, there seems to be little about Ruth West to
> connect her to the glamorous world of show business. She is a
> small dumpling of a woman, warm with shy eyes and a soft
> voice—just what grandmothers are made of. But the next time
> you see such sexy stars as Ann-Margret, the Jacksons, Bobbi
> Gentry, the Temptations or the Fifth Dimension, they just
> might be wearing "the Ruth West look."
>
>

"Name it. She'll Make It!"
by Louie Robinson,
Ebony (May 1977)
>

Endings

Article leads are crucially important, but an article's ending, too, must be carefully planned and written. Far too

often, articles simply peter out, as if the writer's interest in his subject had flagged. An effective ending may offer one final perception, a new insight that keeps the reader thinking about the article long after he has finished reading it.

In a piece about Frank Lloyd Wright, in *Saturday Review,* author Pedro E. Guerroro—who, because he is primarily a photographer, thinks visually—leaves his reader with a memorable image. He tells how, on his last visit to Wright's winter home, Taliesen West in Arizona, only a few weeks before the great architect's death in 1965 at the age of 92,

> Mr. Wright and I went for a long stroll in the desert, plotting angles for some helicopter photographs. His stride was as brisk as the spring air, and I honestly thought he would live forever.

Lynn Sherr concluded an article entitled "How Much Money Do You Earn?" (*Working Woman,* April 1977) as follows:

> As workers, I suppose we owe it to each other to stop pretending we make more, or less, than we really do. As women workers, we probably have a special obligation to liberate our paychecks from societal taboos. But I think it will be difficult. I had planned to end this article by telling you how much I am getting paid to write it. I have changed my mind. I'm not there yet. I'm afraid I really think it's none of your business.

A long *Atlantic Monthly* profile (July 1975) of the unquenchable Armand Hammer, 77-year-old founder and chief executive of the fast-growing Occidental Petroleum Company, concludes: "He knows he can't continue forever. He knows he's mortal. But he's an optimist."

Julia Benjamin closed her article on the new interest in exorcism ("Satan: Alive and Well?", *Saturday Evening Post,* April 1977) with this provocative paragraph:

> The devil was so real to Martin Luther that he hurled an inkwell at him. Is there a devil? "Resist him for a week," suggests an elderly priest, "and you will find out."

An article in *Audubon* (January 1976) on Currituck Banks, a remote section of North Carolina shoreland that has recently been threatened by large-scale development, ended in the following way:

> You could walk yourself weary along the beach picking up shells or prowl through the woods and dunes botanizing and birdwatching and maybe scaring yourself half to death when you encountered a feral hog with two-inch tusks. You could do all these things and others without any fear, for you knew that in all those hours and miles you would never come across any sign that told you not to do this or to buy that, or encounter any living thing as voracious or as greedy as your fellow man.
>
> > "Fare-Thee-Well, Currituck Banks,"
> > by Gary Soucie

Recap and summary

The ending can serve as a summary or capsule recapitulation of the article itself, as in the following, quoted from a *Woman's Day* article on the all-too-common problem of wife-beating ("The Wife Beaters," by Susan Edmiston):

> Ultimately, the solution to this problem must come from changes in a society that makes it almost impossible for a woman to refuse to tolerate abuse. But for now, each battered woman faces the immensely difficult problem of what to do. Her situation cannot change unless she does something about it.

Whether she chooses to leave her husband, to convince him to seek counseling with her or to take a stand against the use of violence in her home and back it up with the willingness to leave, her course is not an easy one. But for the first time her problem *is* being discussed, she knows she is not alone and hope is finally at hand.

"How TV Cops Flout the Law" was the title of a hard-hitting blast at television crime shows, published in *Saturday Review*. Its summary conclusion read as follows:

> The line between television logic, police logic and judicial logic is becoming all but indiscernible. The ideological tension between security and liberty seems to have diminished, very much to the disadvantage of liberty. For television, the challenge is how to give sane, constitutional values access to the TV crime scene. Meanwhile, sad to say, our study of television police dramas indicates that a very dubious type of police logic is in clear control of the airwaves.

There are, as we have seen, many different ways of starting and finishing articles. With a compelling beginning and an ending that, one way or another, reverberates in the reader's mind, an article stands a far better chance of success—with editor and reader—than if it starts prosaically and concludes with no particular emphasis. Practice developing leads and endings; study those that seem to you to be particularly effective, and try to figure out why they are successful. Your growing skill in these important areas will attract readers and keep them watching for your articles.

~10~

The Body of the Article

As important as a compelling lead and an ending with impact is the flesh and blood of the piece—the body. This major part of the article the writer must develop, usually from the notes he has carefully jotted down (with sources) during his research, interviews and background reading.

Basically there are three ways to flesh out an article:

1. By directly quoting authorities, whose qualifications should be indicated.

2. By the use of statistics, descriptive detail, scraps of dialogue and quoted remarks, bits of factual data drawn from reference sources.

3. Through use of anecdotal material that supports and illustrates the theme.

In any given article one or all of these methods may be used. Art of living and personality pieces usually rely heavily on anecdotal and descriptive material, while a fact piece is more likely to include lots of statistical information and authoritative quotes. But illustrative anecdotes and dramatic incidents can be useful in fact articles, too. A *New*

York Times Magazine piece on new methods of forecasting earthquakes had as its lead a brief but dramatic description of the quake that shook the town of New Madrid, Missouri, back in 1811, rerouting the Mississippi River and creating a 10-mile-long lake where no lake had been before. The graphic picture prepares the reader to accept the need for accurate forecasting, especially since he is told that except in California most U.S. construction does not, even now, conform to codes designed to mitigate quake damage.

In contrast with the earthquake piece, one on rent control in New York City, also in the *Times Magazine,* peppers the reader with facts and figures from past and present (e.g., "During the past five years the number of housing units in the city has dropped for the first time since New York was burned by retreating Americans in 1776," "a third of a century of rent control retained in the pockets of tenants $20 billion that otherwise would have been paid to landlords.").

Statistical evidence is drawn from other cities as well as New York, with figures on population decline in Chicago, Boston, Philadelphia and San Francisco used to show that rent control alone was not the cause of New York's brush with bankruptcy. All the facts and figures, informative in themselves, provide convincing groundwork for the writer's reluctant conclusion that rent control must go. Without statistics, the piece would be just an expression of opinion; with them it is a well-reasoned argument likely to be quoted whenever the subject is discussed in the weeks and months following the article's publication.

Statistics are useful, even in a light-hearted profile like *Newsweek's* tribute to Metropolitan tenor Luciano Pavarotti (also known, *Newsweek* tells us, as Lucky, Lurch, and Deep Throat). To support the statement that "Pavarotti is the biggest turn-on in opera" (the article's theme), the magazine reports: "The Pavarotti people have bought more than a half million copies of his five solo records and eleven opera albums, putting joy in his heart and adding substantially to his annual income, which is close to a half million dollars."

Techniques that work

Here again, techniques of fiction are often needed to hold the reader's attention and interest from start to finish. Descriptive detail, dialogue, dramatic incident—all these fit into the framework of an article, lending color and credibility. Anecdotal material, the very stuff of fiction, is invaluable. To quote Webster again, the anecdote is "a usually short narrative of an interesting, amusing or curious incident, often biographical and generally characterized by human interest."

Thus an anecdote by definition adds an element of zest to the text, a human-interest touch that helps to bring the article to life. Used at the start, as in some of the leads quoted earlier, anecdotes bring people into the picture right away, and people are as important in articles as they are in photographs. (Virginia Woolf said, in a letter to a young writer, "I don't see how to write a book without people in it.")

Almost inevitably, in a biographical piece, the anecdote adds a little to the characterization (it's probably not worth using if it doesn't). Don Guy closed his article about his "Neighbor Aiken" (*Yankee*, October 1975), the Vermont Senator, with an anecdote:

As we started to depart by backing around the driveway flanked by the thriving vegetable garden, retired Senator George David Aiken leaned towards our car. We paused for one last word of wisdom from the former dean of the Senate.

"Don't worry about hitting those turnips. I planted them on the edge because I really don't like turnips."

A revealing anecdote in the profile of the great tenor, Pavarotti, referred to his taste for pretty girls:

As a toucher and grabber, he reached his finest hour in a performance of "Rigoletto" at the Met, when he manhandled mezzo-soprano Joanne Grillo as if she were Galatea. "Naturally I try to put my hand in her dress," Pavarotti explains. "I tell to her I don't touch her as Mr. Pavarotti but as the Duke of Mantua. But she is thinking all wrong." Recalls Grillo: "I hit him on the head with my whip. That evening is one of my fondest memories."

The article goes on to explain that Pavarotti has a strong sense of morality: "To be great you must be good. Music by itself is not enough. . .," he is quoted as saying.

Anecdotes do not usually—and should not—spring full blown from the writer's imagination. Although some fictionizing is legitimate in certain kinds of articles, and names of people and places can and often should be changed, anecdotes are more convincing and effective if they are basically factual. (They *must* be true if real persons are named or identifiable and, even if true, may be ruled out by the magazine's counsel, always nervous about the possibility of libel or invasion of privacy litigation.)

The techniques of fiction were successfully employed in a 20-page *Reader's Digest* article on the production and distribution of oil, a strictly factual subject if ever there was one.

But roving editor Nathan Adams imposed a shape on his unwieldy material by starting off the complicated story with a casual observation by a gasoline customer, mentioned by name and identified as living in Coral Springs, Florida. Customer Lee Rinderman's words were: "It's a miracle," and Adams relates them to the production of the "Tankful of Gas" that flowed into her car, tracing its origin back millions of years to the ancient water hole where the oil developed, then on through the ages to present-day Saudi Arabia and thence, by VLCC (Very Large Crude Carrier) *Edinburgh* to Freeport, oil transfer port in the Bahamas, then by smaller ship to the refinery at Pascagoula and then on to Port Everglades, the marketing terminal that serves the Florida gas station where our heroine regularly purchases gasoline for her red Pontiac sedan. At key points in the story, dialogue is employed:

> "How does it go, Budrovic?" Ovidth [the *Edinburgh* captain] asked.
> "Sixty thousand barrels an hour," the officer answered. "We're loading Five Starboard Tank."
> "When do we finish?"
> Budrovic shrugged. "Maybe by seven tomorrow morning."

The vast size of the cargo is thus impressed upon the reader.

Throughout there are flashbacks to Mrs. Lee Rinderman's barrel of oil and to the Standard of Kentucky service station of the opening scene. Thus, the reader follows for some twenty pages of text, the progress of that specific shipment to its destination, and a certain element of suspense is introduced in what might otherwise have been a dully informative recitation of facts about the oil industry. All through the article, the detailed description is accurate and image-evoking:

> Barren deserts like the Rub' al Khali—the 250,000-square-mile "Empty Quarter"—reach as far as the eye can see. The *shamals*, the windstorms of spring, bring little moisture. But they curve the dunes into towering waves of sand that roll to the horizon . . .
>
> Beyond the slate-colored swells, the early morning sun shone on the city of Cape Town and on the mists that flow like cream down the slopes of Table Mountain . . .
>
> At 8:45, Chief Officer Budrovic ordered the engine room to start *Edinburgh*'s hugh discharge pumps. In the control room, the display panel light suddenly glowed red and green . . .

"A Tankful of Gas," by Nathan M. Adams, appeared in the May 1976 issue of *The Reader's Digest*. As a demonstration of effective magazine writing, it merits study by anyone interested in producing readable and at the same time accurately informative articles on subjects of real significance in today's world.

In "A Field Guide to Roger Tory Peterson," an article published in *American Artist* (April 1977), writer John Diffily supported his contention that the famed ornithologist is, above all, an artist by including everything his research had produced that bore on his subject's compulsion to draw and paint. "At age eleven, Peterson was introduced to Audubon Society leaflets that presented portraits of birds from which the student drew and colored his own." During his high school days he found work decorating furniture with scrolls and baroque curlicues, meanwhile saving money for art school in New York. The article continues, always with emphasis on Peterson's development as an artist. But the author gives him full credit also for devising a system for field identification of birds, a concept "of pure genius" that has brought him world renown. Before then descriptions were written by academicians who thought verbally. "Peterson, an artist, was visual." The article goes on, bringing to readers of the art magazine in which it appeared a good deal of detailed information on bird identification along with a new recognition of Roger Tory Peterson's artistic status and the methods he employs in painting his feathered subjects.

Perhaps these examples are enough to indicate how research material can and must always be drawn on to provide an article's substance. Small descriptive and factual details add to an article's readability and, just as important, to its credibility. We *believe* the writer who tells us not only what happened, but also what the persons involved in the piece looked like, how they spoke and against what specific background the action took place. These, the reader subconsciously realizes, are not things the writer is likely to make up out of whole cloth. Similarly, photographic illustration adds to believability. If photos are available, send a few along with the manuscript, if only to help convince the editor of your truthfulness and attention to detail.

Make the most of your research material. It is from those notes, laboriously taken in the library and during interviews, that you will draw the bones and body of your article.

~ 11 ~

Digging Out the Facts

As we have seen, research is the very essence of the fact article. Although the way the material is handled and the actual writing of the article are also important, thorough research is the ground on which the factual article stands.

Curiosity rather than specialized knowledge is the factual writer's stock in trade. Most of us aren't really authorities on much of anything. Even writers of highly authoritative works on abstruse subjects must dig out their facts from published sources, interviews, research papers, etc. What is needed before undertaking a factual article is mainly a keen desire to know more about the proposed topic.

Using libraries

Research cannot be skimped and it is time-consuming. Once you have decided on your subject and have at least a tentative idea of how you will approach it, make the library your work place for a while. Most public libraries have standard reference works and, if you are lucky, a file of major periodicals. There may be a college or university in your area with a more extensive reference collection. While borrowing privileges in college libraries are ordinarily limited to students and faculty, the librarian will usually permit others to use books and reference materials at the library.

Specialized topics and materials can be tracked down through the numerous indexes of periodicals in special fields. These specialized indexes can lead you to valuable source material or previous coverage of your general subject. There are indexes to professional publications in art, science, industry, technology, business, education and the like, with articles listed by subject, author and title and the publications they appeared in identified by name and date. The larger libraries usually have either bound volumes or, more commonly now, microfilms of back issues. Microfilmed material is used in the library with a scanner, now generally available in reference departments.

Most libraries also have on their shelves the regularly published listings of government publications on a host of topics in almost any field you can think of. These can generally be obtained at nominal cost through the office of the Superintendent of Documents, Washington, D.C. 20402. You can also ask to have your name put on the mailing list to receive new listings in a particular field. Public libraries subscribe to the same service and often buy pamphlets on subjects of current or general interest to place on their reference shelves.

Information sources

The public relations departments of all large companies, of government agencies, non-profit organizations, city administrations, and even public school systems are all ready to be cooperative if approached in a friendly way.

The government extension services, with offices located in county seats, operate under the Department of Agriculture. They are veritable gold mines of information on anything pertaining to farming, gardening, landscaping, pest control, (indoors and out) and conservation, as well as aspects of homemaking and personal finance.

Who's Who and *Who Was Who* are useful for checking names and dates of outstanding people, but *Biography Index* is a much richer source of references to published articles about people who have figured in the news. *Current Biography,* issued monthly and compiled every year, offers detailed, often quite colorful sketches of successful individuals, usually including anecdotal material in addition to straight biographical data.

When in the course of your research you come on references to magazines or books not to be found in your local library, you can obtain help from the librarian, who may be able to borrow them for you through your state's inter-library loan service. On occasion it may be worthwhile to travel some distance in order to use the facilities of your state's biggest and best library, typically located in the state capital.

The Library of Congress in Washington receives, under the Copyright Law of the United States, two copies of each and every book published in this country and stores many historical documents and memorabilia. Obscure titles and out-of-print books can always be consulted there. If you are too far away from Washington to drop in at the great institution that houses the national book collection, it is usually possible to have chapters or specified pages Xeroxed for a small fee. For only a modest sum, one can obtain photocopies of entire out-of-print books and historic documents from the Library of Congress. A similar service for books published in Great Britain is provided by the Public Record Office, Chancery Lane, London. Most public libraries in the United States provide photocopy service *if* you can give them the specific reference, although the newly revised copyright law places definite restrictions on photocopying of material still in copyright and may therefore affect library photocopy services to a considerable extent.

Reference checks

Besides the obviously specialized sources of information, a truly indispensable and readily available reference found in every library is *The Readers' Guide to Periodical Literature,* a regularly published listing of articles and short fiction published in all the general and many of the more specialized magazines. Before undertaking to write an article or query an editor about it, you should check the *Readers' Guide* for references to your subject. It would be foolish to approach the editor of *Sports Illustrated,* for example, with a detailed query on an article about Muhammad Ali or Billie Jean King if that magazine published a full-length profile of your proposed subject only a few months ago. A long list of *Readers' Guide* references to recent articles in a variety of magazines on the subject of transcendental meditation, shall we say, or health foods, yoga, bicycling, weight-lifting or how to buy a used car might be your tip to steer clear of these topics until the overconcentration of coverage dies down, and there is a better chance of editorial interest in fresh, up-to-date treatments of them.

The more specific your subject, the more important it is not to overlook any reference to it in the magazine you plan to approach. If you find one, try to check it out. Perhaps the overlap is not too serious after all. But in proposing the subject you should indicate to the editor your awareness of previous coverage and point out how your projected piece will amplify it or, perhaps, present the material from a new angle.

Some subjects are covered in magazine articles year after year, but from different angles or with new information. A garden magazine might publish an article every year on the new varieties of flowers and vegetables the seed companies have introduced that year. A magazine like *American Home* reports on new products available to do-it-yourself home-owners and new ways of using them. (Though this type of informational material is often staff-written, a fresh news-worthy item may be accepted if the timing is right.)

Keeping notes and records

As you go through the references to your subject, take notes, keeping careful record of the sources of those notes for checking purposes later on. Direct quotes must always be accurately attributed. You'll save time if you record your sources fully as you do the research instead of having to race back to the library to recheck every time you want to use a quote.

Assessing your facts

Digging out material for a substantial article can be a lot of fun. Indeed, writers have been known to get so deeply involved in the long search for material that they never wrote the article. Like the permanent Ph.D. candidate who can never complete his thesis, these writers suffer from research-itis. The article writer, not himself a scholar, must go beyond his research to the crucially important job of shaping an article, finding out just what the mass of facts he has assembled means and what may be their significance to the reader. While there may be room in a book for tangential material, the article writer must learn to discard ruthlessly everything not clearly related to the subject.

Research takes many forms. For some articles, there may be family records, old correspondence, recollections of older family members to draw on. Attics sometimes yield treasures in the form of old magazine and newspaper files, dated pictures showing period costumes, photographs of local areas in an earlier era, perhaps before fires destroyed the town's center and larger modern buildings replaced the original wooden structures. An attic treasure like the one discovered by a Radcliffe student not long ago and widely reported in the newspapers doesn't turn up often. The young woman's great-grandmother collected first-person reports from hundreds of pioneer women. Stored for years in a trunk, these handwritten reports will surely provide raw material for one or more articles, perhaps even a book that could contribute significantly to the ongoing discussion of women's role in our world.

Article writer Jeremy Dole made good (if tongue-in-cheek) use of yellowed correspondence he unearthed in the attic of his family's Vermont house—an exchange of letters between poet Robert Frost and Dole's grandfather, who ran the hardware store in the town where Frost lived. The letters concerned Frost's refusal to pay for an ice cream freezer, because it allegedly made inferior ice cream, and Dole's grandfather's insistence that he should get his money for the freezer he had sold to Frost. The article, impressively titled "The Frost-Hoblin Papers," was published in the Vermont-based magazine, *Country Journal.*

If your family has lived in the same house for generations, the closets, attic and cellar of the house may well yield treasure that can be turned into marketable magazine articles. If, for instance, you should decide to write a profile of your distinguished grandfather, you would probably want to include a sketch of his childhood. Your recollections of the man, who may have died while you were still a child, would be greatly enhanced were you to find pictures and snapshots of him in the house. His day-to-day journals, letters he wrote or clippings of material he contributed to the local newspaper, yellowed clippings of stories about him, even long-paid bills and checkbooks, if still extant, would comprise valuable primary source material. If relatives who knew your grandfather better than you did are still alive, you will want to interview them.

In gathering this potentially excellent material for your profile, make sure to avoid the cataloguing of detail that writers sometimes get bogged down in. Instead, work your background material in deftly to convince your readers that you know your subject inside out, without boring them with a dull recital of your newly acquired knowledge. Balance is needed here, balance and good judgment, a certain sense of good taste that tells a writer when to stop if he is to avoid putting his readers to sleep.

Painful though it may be, it is often necessary to set aside or delete material that is good but not pertinent to the article you are working on. Take heart. Those bits of local color, anecdotes and other fascinating information you cannot find a place for in the project at hand may be usable later on in other articles. In researching one article, you may find enough material for several different kinds of pieces that will sell to publications with differing editorial requirements, emphasis, treatment, approach, and length. Occasionally, an investigation proves to be so fascinating, the sources of information so rich, that the writer goes on to develop a book on a subject first presented in magazine article form.

You can never tell in advance just where research will lead. The honest writer must be prepared to abandon an article that research reveals as untrue or without value; conversely, his investigation sometimes uncovers riches that suggest there is material for a longer work in what he originally looked on as an article subject.

In at least one case I know of, the writer's unsuccessful effort to compress within the confines of a *Reader's Digest*-length article material that demanded—and deserved—book-length treatment finally resulted in an outstanding work of nonfiction. Rex Allen Smith's *Moon of Popping Trees* is a book that exemplifies the creative use of what the author himself described as "a burden of research" conducted in his attempt to write a magazine article.

Files, devices, memory cues

No matter what kind of article you work on, a personal filing system of some sort can be extremely helpful. Folders of clippings, notes for future articles, references to books and magazines, arranged under broad subject headings (Education, Gardening, Home Improvement, Sports, Business, Exploration, Children, etc.) will build up gradually so that when you start work on a specific subject, you will have right in your own files a considerable amount of background material to look over.

Notebooks are standard equipment for writers, useful in many ways. Our view of the world around us changes from day to day and year to year, changes more than we realize.

It is a good idea to jot down impressions, descriptive bits about the weather, observations of people and places, quotes that seem memorable. Memory has a marvelous capacity for failure. To forestall such failures, a writer should put thoughts to paper almost as they occur. Thornton Wilder pinned notes to himself on a bulletin board in his study to help him retain details that came to mind for later use in the book he was working on. Even a writer with an excellent memory (an attribute whose value can hardly be overestimated) sometimes needs cues to jog his recollections of people, places and events. To such a writer, lengthy note-taking may not be necessary, but a brief daily record of activities (and regular notation of engagements and expenses) is certain to prove useful in many ways.

Another way of accumulating article material is by talking with people who know more about your subject than you do—or know it in a different, first-hand sort of way. In the first instance, you'll get the sort of authoritative quote from an "expert" that is almost always a part of medical articles in the general magazines—a doctor's statement, for example. In preparing an article for *Today's Health* (since merged with *Family Health*) on "What Your Hands Tell a Doctor about Your Health," author Don Schanche interviewed several doctors who gave their views about the hand as medical indicator. Schanche's own physician's opinions on the subject provided him with the conclusion for his article. At the end of a physical checkup, the doctor examined the author's fingers one by one, commenting:

You've been smoking again, haven't you?" he asked, disapprovingly.

"How can you tell?" I asked him. "My fingers aren't tobacco-stained."

"Smoking constricts the blood vessels of the extremities," he said. "It can lower the skin temperature of your fingers by 5 to 15 degrees. So can pain, anger, fear and doing arithmetic, but since you're not doing any of those right now, I assume you must have been smoking. Your fingers are like ice."

After checking me out from head to toe the doctor gave me an almost clean bill of health. "There's just one thing," he said.

"What's that?" I asked, with apprehension.

"STOP SMOKING. You won't listen to me, but your hands are trying to tell you something. Listen to them."

Sometimes what you need is not "authority" as such, but anecdotal and illustrative material with the impact of first-hand experience. Adroitly woven into the factual material, a half dozen such anecdotes or illustrations and examples can make up most of the content of an article. Though the individual writer probably cannot conduct a formal survey, quotes and examples collected through conversations with friends, neighbors and local "experts," and letters to people in other parts of the country who, there is reason to believe, may have something to contribute, can provide the case material you need for an article dealing with a problem encountered by many people.

One such problem might be the increasing tendency of young men and women to live openly together before (or instead of) marriage. Wise counsel on how to handle this quite prevalent situation would be welcomed by anxious parents across the country. Ways to give psychological support to someone facing terminal illness, how to help aging parents adjust to retirement or loss of mate, how to ease a friend's adjustment to crippling illness or injury, are other problems many readers may have to face in their lives.

Drawing on material collected in your personal investigation, with added quotes from experts, found either in print or through interviews, you will be able to put together an article that, if sensitively narrated, would not be difficult to sell to a magazine, even though the subject has been done previously by other writers. For basic human problems are of perennial, as well as universal, interest. Readers find comfort and sometimes guidance and direction in articles that tell how others faced problems that in their own lives seem insurmountable, and offer practical, well-researched information on how to cope with them.

The impact of an article is a subtle and complex mix of a variety of elements, not the least of which is the writer's ability to set the scene and bring to life, in a very few words and phrases, the persons who figure importantly in the piece. The reader must be able to see in his mind's eye where the action is taking place, and he can do so only with the writer's effective and skillful use of fictional devices. Thorough research will provide the detail you need to sketch accurately the background of the events described and put flesh on the bones of the people involved in them. Here is where you will use the specifics you have dug up in interviews and in the library. Use just enough to identify "characters" and recreate the scene, making it a believable backdrop for the action.

People are always interesting. In interviews and casual conversations, learn to watch closely, to listen as people speak, not only to their words but for the sound of their voices. Record in your ever-present notebook what you hear—bits of dialogue, colorful phrases, colloquialisms—as well as any generalizations that may result from your observations. Practice reproducing overheard voices on paper, sketching in words the faces of people who impress you and recording their speech. These brief vignettes will bring the people back to you later. Watch for significant elements of appearance. Like the short story writer, you must present your major characters in the round, and since you are writing nonfiction, the details must be accurate and in strict accord with the facts. Practice noting eye and hair color, clothing, height, type of build, etc. The reader cannot supply this information as he reads unless you first give it to him.

Not all the details will stay in the final version, but enough should to ensure that the article has what editors call "substance." When the article must depend entirely on published sources (as a biography of an historical figure or re-enactment of some significant happening in the past), dig deep enough into peripheral source material of the period to find the kind of descriptive detail needed to bring your subject to life.

~12~

Queries
When and How to Write Them

Editors of major magazines and of specialized publications often require writers to send query letters before submitting manuscripts for consideration. Many of the smaller publications also want writers to query first and to submit their articles only if they get a go-ahead from the editor. But there are other magazines—and this includes some large and well-paying ones—that prefer to have the writer submit the article without prior query, so that it can be considered immediately and accepted or rejected without delay.

The attitude of the various publications toward query letters is indicated in their listings in *The Writer* or *The Writer's Handbook.* In general it is prudent to query in advance if considerable research is going to be required for the piece you are thinking of writing. Although the beginning writer is not likely to get a firm commitment, even from an editor who reacts favorably to his proposal, a query will at least eliminate the possibility of duplicating a project the magazine already has under way. Further, the initial query, if it is provocative and catches the editor's interest,

may bring suggestions for shaping the article to conform more closely to the particular magazine's editorial
requirements.

Some research will very likely be needed before writing
the query, for you want it to sound authoritative and to
indicate not only the subject matter, in capsule form, but
the point of view that will be developed and the overall
thrust of the projected article. The editor's response to your
query will determine how much more research you need to
do and may suggest the article's specific focus. Once you get
some encouragement for your idea, you will be ready to
proceed.

Whether or not the editor offers suggestions for handling
the material, you should keep in mind the kind of audience
you are aiming for and frame your article accordingly. In an
article of prime interest to older readers, planned for submission to *Modern Maturity,* for example, it would hardly
be suitable to include contemporary slang expressions or
"in" references to the youth counterculture, references that
would surely be either offensive or incomprehensible to
members of the American Association of Retired Persons
for whom the magazine is published.

Obviously, you will consider sending queries only to
those publications you know from market lists to be open
markets for free-lance writers and not, as is the case in some
instances, substantially or entirely staff written. You will
want to become familiar with as many magazines as possible, either by writing for sample copies or by spending time
regularly in the periodicals room of your public library,
examining the large variety of magazines there. Notes identi-
fying certain authors as free-lance writers indicate that a
magazine uses free-lance material and may be worth query-

ing, if you have a piece you think would fit its editorial format.

Even if a magazine does not regularly publish a statement of its editorial needs, you can address a query to the editor—or to the articles editor, when one is listed on the masthead. Presumably the magazine will be one you have read at least occasionally. It is important to know your market and to have a feel for the kind of article published by the particular magazine you are querying, and the treatment it seems to prefer. (An article writer really should be an habitual magazine reader!)

"Salesman" by mail

The query, remember, is essentially a sales letter. Make it as persuasive and provocative as you can, including if possible your lead for the article and summarizing the material you plan to cover. Your query should also give the sources of information available to you. While the whole query need be no more than two or three pages long, you will be well advised to work hard on it, making sure it is well-written and neatly typed, contains no misspelled words or grammatical errors and is a cogent summary of your projected article. The editor who reads the query should receive a clear impression of the subject proposed, presented in a way that will make him curious to read more about it.

Sometimes this can be done in outline form, but the outline must be sufficiently detailed to convey clearly the shape of the projected article and some of your excitement about the subject and why you feel that it is important. Ordinarily, the proposal will be most effectively presented in the less restricted letter form. The letter's opening might actually be the first paragraph of the article as you plan to write it, especially if you have found a really good anecdote to lead off with. A rough summary of the content will follow, with an indication of your qualifications for writing the piece and an estimate of its finished length.

The form a query takes will depend to a certain extent on whether or not the writer has had prior dealings with the editor to whom it is addressed. The beginner, querying an editor for the first time, must not only present the subject he wants to cover but also make it clear that he is qualified to do such an article. Once he is known to the editor, the formalities can be dispensed with and attention focused on the article itself.

In detailing qualifications, it will be helpful to list your writing "credits" (if any) or your educational and job background, especially as these pertain to the proposed subject. Karl Kristofferson, a writer not known to *The Reader's Digest* when he first queried the editors about an article on the Pioneer 10 space program, had been doing public relations work for NASA for several years and was closely connected with the Apollo launchings. He was living at the time near Cape Canaveral and, for that reason and because of the nature of his work, had ready access to information (unclassified, of course) needed to develop an article on this highly technical subject. Working and living in the midst of space development as he was, Kristofferson's excitement about the space flights was real and persuasive. He was given a provisional go-ahead (without commitment), and proceeded to develop the piece that appeared in the *Digest* (September 1972) under the title "First Voyage to the Stars."

Karl Kristofferson has since sold *The Reader's Digest* articles on the Mariner probe of Mars ("Voyage to the Red

Planet," October 1973) and one that reported observations
of the planet Jupiter ("The Amazing Voyage of Pioneer
10," May 1974). In proposing these later articles, the space
writer did not need to go into lengthy detail about his qualifications, by then well established in the minds of the *Digest*
editors. His effective query letter proposing the piece on
Mars was considerably longer and more detailed than the
excerpts quoted below:

> Dear . . .
> I have an idea you might want to consider. I call it A New
> Look at an "Old" Planet.
> Even as Pioneer 10 was winging its way toward the stars,
> another unmanned spaceship aptly named Mariner 9 was giving
> the planet Mars the once over. The results are now in, and they
> are quite startling.
> Six months ago, the world's astronomers were convinced that
> Mars, like the moon, was geologically dead. Previous Mariner
> excursions to the red planet in 1965 and 1969 had returned
> pictures of a crater-filled world devoid of water, faint traces of
> an atmosphere, and little hope for life in any form, past, present
> or future.
> What emerged from Mariner's photographs is a dramatic new
> picture of a "dead" planet. Here was a world where gigantic
> volcanoes erupt, oozing out floods of molten rock; where on
> most afternoons wispy clouds float above the mountains; where
> incredible winds can create sandstorms that engulf an entire
> world; where the forces that move continents have opened up a
> planetary crevice that dwarfs the earth's Grand Canyon.

Kristofferson's well-written and informative letter went
on in this vein for another page or so, concluding:

> The true story of Mars will not be known until much later.
> Russian and American unmanned spaceships scheduled to land

on the Martian surface in a year or so may solve some of the riddles. But the final chapter will be written only when man himself sets foot on the mysterious red planet. One thing is certain: No one in the scientific community is ready to write Mars off as a dead planet any longer, thanks to Mariner 9.

Are you interested? Then let me supply you with a good, overall story that explores the Mariner 9 mission and its epic discoveries.

Kristofferson got an assignment, and "Voyage to the Red Planet" was the result.

If possible, address your query to an editor *by name,* checking the magazine's masthead to identify the articles editor, if one is listed, or address the editor of the specialized department for which your article is intended. The various directories of magazines and market lists—*The Writer's Handbook, Literary Market Place, Gebbie Press All-in-One Directory, Ayer Directory of Publications, Standard Periodical Directory* and others—contain such information, but it is always best to examine a copy of the magazine itself if one is obtainable.

Bear in mind that your query is the first sample of your writing the editor will see and you will be judged by it. Spare no pains to make it a favorable reflection of your style, attitude and command of language. Lead off, if possible, with the best anecdote your preliminary research has turned up. If you have a compelling personal interest in the subject, make that fact clear and tell what lies behind it. This may be a part of the article and will at any rate convince the editor of your real concern or enthusiasm.

An article today cannot be a simple cataloguing of facts but must come to a conclusion or reflect a particular point of view. Only if your own thinking and research have

reached the point where you know—or think you know—
what it all means to you and why the article should be
written now can you convey the facts and their significance
in an orderly and compelling way. The clearer you are, at
the query stage, about the shape the article will take, the
more likely you are to receive a favorable response from the
editor.

A lifelong devotion to the art of ballet, for example,
might suddenly take on new meaning for you upon reading
of the "dance boom" now taking place in this country.
Perhaps, you might think, this is the year to transform that
until now dilettante interest into a salable article on some
aspect of the dance scene. But what aspect? That is the
question you will want to decide before framing your query
letter. Are you primarily concerned with dance as a possible
avocation for your child? Has your own recent experience
with a dance class been so rewarding you feel compelled to
spread the news? Or has some one dance personality cap-
tured your fancy? An elderly friend of mind recently sold
Dance Magazine a piece that capsulized her vivid recollections of one memorable day back in the twenties when she
picnicked with Isadora Duncan in the countryside outside
of Paris.

It isn't enough to tell the editor of *Dogs Magazine* in a
query that you want to do an article on dog training. He
will want to know right at the start what you propose to
say on the subject, what authority you have for your opinions, whether you support the behavioral approach or
advocate traditional methods of discipline, how you yourself feel about dogs, what experience you have had with
them and what avenues of research you propose to follow.
He may not ask these questions, but unless your query

letter encompasses this sort of information, you'll very likely receive a prompt "no, thank you" in response.

Although further research and the actual writing of the article may change its direction somewhat, it is at the query stage that a tentative decision should be reached on the overall "pitch" of the piece. It is important, too, to explain in your query letter why right now is the time to begin work on the article in order to have it ready a few months hence—perhaps to coincide with events that will make it timely then.

Many of us have never had the opportunity to develop the sort of technical expertise a medical or space writer needs, but almost everyone has some one area in which he or she can claim special knowledge or experience. Your consuming passion for tennis, golf or horseback riding, the fascination that woodworking, rug hooking or ceramics hold for you or your rewarding experience as a volunteer—in hospital, school or institution for the retarded—may qualify you to write on these or comparable subjects.

Still another sort of qualification stems from being on the scene when exciting events take place. Convinced that a near-tragedy in his hometown in Florida had the makings of a dramatic true story, sports writer Frank Sargeant queried *The Reader's Digest* as follows:

> At 2 p.m. on a sunny Sunday afternoon, Glenda Lennon was swept to sea. The shallow waters off Homosassa, Florida, are not particularly treacherous. But when no sign of the 23-year-old diver was found throughout the night, tragedy appeared certain.
>
> Despite the odds, one man believed he could find her. Aging marina operator Duncan MacRae joined the search early Monday morning. And "with the grace of God and a little mathe-

matics," the old seaman led rescuers 18 miles into the Gulf of Mexico, directly to the struggling girl. Miraculously, Glenda was still swimming, more than 20 hours after leaving her boat.

I believe Glenda's heroic swim and MacRae's remarkable navigation would make an interesting story for your readers. Many aspects of the rescue are highly dramatic.

The young woman's husband, Robert, was a high school swimming star. But when he tried to save her, he was locked in a muscle-cramping six-hour struggle with the eight knot current himself. Glenda's dog, Spunky, leaped into the water when he saw his mistress in trouble, only to perish when she finally had to release him to save herself. She survived the night in shark-infested waters without any flotation device, relying only on a snorkel, swim mask and flippers to keep her alive.

Thunder storms rolled around her in the blackness. A rescue plane dropped a flare within a few hundred feet of her, but she was not seen. She fought a constant battle with fatigue, often falling asleep to be shocked awake when water filled her swim mask. And through it all, she could not know whether or not her husband had survived his own ordeal.

If you are interested, I'd like to send along a 3000-word narrative on the rescue. I'll include quotes from Glenda, her husband, MacRae and others on the rescuing boat, and U.S. Coast Guard rescue teams. I personally hold a guide's license for Florida's central Gulf Coast and have a thorough knowledge of the area of the search.

I believe I can turn in a compact, fast-moving piece that will re-create the drama of that long night and give insight into the faith and courage of those who lived it.

That letter, addressed simply to the editors (Mr. Sargeant was unknown to the *Digest* when his query arrived), was read and commented on favorably by two members of the editorial staff. Within a day or so, one of them sent off a reply expressing keen interest in seeing a 3,000-word piece on the rescue of Glenda Lennon. No commitment was made, but Frank Sargeant went ahead with the project on speculation. The manuscript lived up to the editors' expectations. Additional information was requested by telephone and promptly supplied by the author. The *Digest* accepted the piece and sent a check off to Sargeant. The article, published in the magazine under the title, "Glenda's Long, Lonely Swim," proved to be one of the most popular in the issue and was reprinted in all the *Digest's* overseas editions.

Another try

If your first query proves unproductive, *don't give up.* Try the same idea elsewhere. If that doesn't work and you still believe you have a good idea for an article, then go ahead and write it anyhow. You will do your best job with a subject you feel strongly about, for feeling is an important element in good writing, be it fiction or nonfiction. If you believe in it, be willing to speculate.

It might be a good idea, though, to consider first why several editors have failed to warm to the proposal. You may, of course, have picked the wrong magazines. Another reason why your query has not been encouraged could be that the subject has been done to death from various angles in magazines that reach large numbers of people. Checking *The Readers' Guide* will help you avoid this mistake. Or your query letter may simply have failed to suggest the full possibilities of your subject. Spend a day or so strengthening it by adding material, tightening the actual writing and doing everything possible to convey your enthusiasm for the subject. If, after all this, the letter still fails to stir interest, put it aside for a few months. The timing may be wrong. Some subsequent development (you will naturally be watching the papers for pertinent news items) may be what is needed to bring the subject into focus.

~ 13 ~

How to Sell the Articles
You Write

Nothing equals the pleasure and satisfaction writers feel at seeing their work in print. One way to make sure of getting your articles published with some regularity is to establish a working relationship with one of the smaller or more specialized magazines, perhaps one that caters to readers who share a special interest of your own.

We are fortunate to have in the United States a plethora of magazines available for reading and as markets for the work of both established and beginning writers. Instead of aiming all your efforts at the relatively few general magazines (*The Reader's Digest* receives 3,000 or more article manuscripts per month!), make an effort to find other outlets more specifically in line with your individual tastes and particular interests, outlets where the competition from staff and established professional writers is not so tough. Such contacts, once made, can lead not only to repeated publication in the one magazine but to other markets, too, and possibly to reprinting elsewhere of an article first published in the special-interest or trade magazine. If you concentrate your efforts in one field of subject matter, you may be surprised to find how little it takes to make you an "expert" on a subject many people would like to know more about. Before you know it, you'll be flooded with requests for advice on coin collecting, interior decorating, gardening, astrology or whatever the subject your articles cover. Do not scorn smaller markets. The rewards and repercussions of publication there may surprise you.

Careful study of the market is almost certain to pay off. Make sure you read a variety of magazines each month, buying, borrowing or scrounging them from any and all available sources. Set aside one afternoon a week to spend reading periodicals at your local library. Regular checking of the magazines the library receives will familiarize you with their editorial requirements and overall slant. Others can be checked in the homes of friends, and single copies of publications you are particularly interested in can be ordered by mail from the publishers. (Check *Ayer Directory of Publications* for addresses of magazines you can't find in libraries.)

Your library may also have a shelf of individual copies of some of the more specialized magazines. Or you may discover in or near the place you live a dealer in back copies of magazines. Such a shop can prove a veritable gold mine, not only of old publications, fascinating for their historical value and also extremely valuable for reference, but also of not-so-old issues, often available at half their cover price or less, only a few months after publication date.

Most editors will turn down an otherwise well-written article manuscript if the material is out of line with the magazine's editorial character or focus. You will be wasting the editor's time—and yours—if you submit material that would be out of place in the particular magazine approached. To do so reflects your failure to acquaint yourself with the publication before sending the manuscript there.

The more you study the market listings and familiarize yourself with the magazines themselves, the more you will come to see that for any given manuscript there exists a number of potential outlets. Make a list of the magazines to which the article you plan to write or a query on it might be sent. You will probably top your list with the one among the different possibilities that seems likely to pay the most or has the most prestige value (but avoid the majors until your work has won a few acceptances). If you are turned down by the first, you will try the next, remembering always that there are many reasons why a manuscript or an article proposal may be rejected and that failure to place it the first time out—or even the second or third—does not necessarily reflect on its quality. Magazines have commitments of their own, inventories of purchased manuscripts not yet used, tentative arrangements with staff or other regular writers. A first turndown by what seems the likeliest market certainly should not be enough to discourage submission elsewhere.

Good timing

While often beyond the writer's control, timing is of crucial importance because it is a major consideration of magazine editors. Whatever the frequency of issue of a publication—monthly, weekly, quarterly, bimonthly, or whatever—a certain part of almost any magazine's content will be determined by the date on the cover.

It takes time to edit, print, and distribute a magazine. Lead time, the period that reflects that interval, varies from one publication to another, with the monthlies taking longer, the weeklies necessarily less (although the Sunday magazines, published weekly, have a much longer lead time than the news sections of the papers with which they are distributed). A postcard query or a phone call to the editorial office will give information on lead time for you. If you are thinking of sending a Christmas feature, for example, don't waste your time and effort or the editor's by sending in the article the first of December. By then, the Christmas issue of most monthly magazines is already on the newsstands; work on the late winter or early spring issues has begun and material for summer publication is in the planning stage. Your Christmas proposal should have been made four to six months earlier, to allow time for consideration of the query, preparation and submission of the manuscript, editorial comments and suggestions for revision. December is the time to send out queries on articles dealing in a fresh way with summertime activities—swimming, backpacking, summer jobs, tennis, exploring the national parks, summer camps and camp safety, etc.

Annual events like the Kentucky Derby, the Madison Square Garden horse show or the American Kennel Club dog show, the Rose Bowl ,or the Sugar Bowl games, the opening of the baseball season—or important annual holidays like Christmas, Valentine's Day, Washington's Birthday, the Fourth of July, as well as the changing seasons of the year—all lead to a demand for topical articles that must be planned and scheduled several months in advance so that their publication will coincide with the special event, time of observance, or specific date of the holiday. It is, therefore, up to the writer to keep these dates in mind and to offer appropriate material, if he has it, well in advance. The more specialized (or local) the magazine, the more likely it is that it will want close-up coverage—perhaps a background story on a leading contender for Derby victory or of a colorful and successful jockey, for example. The general-interest magazines, Sunday supplements, etc., may be more interested in a somewhat broader treatment, providing the material is fresh, not simply a repetition of what has been published in previous years. Regional or local publications reflect the seasonal and timely activities and events typical of their parts of the country—a fact worth keeping in mind in writing and submitting article material to them.

Writers must be constantly looking ahead and checking their files for clippings, notes and other reminders that were put away last year for possible future use. A tickler file, common in editorial offices, can be useful to the writer, too. Simply take twelve sturdy folders, mark one for each of the twelve months of the year, and arrange them in order. In them stash away all the bits of information, possible story leads, timely newspaper items, etc., that will likely be useful at a later date. Again, remember that you must always be working ahead. Christmas material, then, should be put into the May or June tickler folder. Make a habit of checking the current month's file on a certain day every week so that you won't overlook anything you might have saved for use that month. As you get accustomed to using the tickler, you'll find yourself depending on it more and more, both as an aid to memory and as a source of ideas.

News when it is news

Timing is important in other ways. A newsworthy story can turn up anywhere. If you are fortunate enough to stumble on one by chance, don't delay. Do something about it that very day. Send off a query, if possible to an editor with whom you have had fruitful dealings in the past, asking him to note your interest in the subject—or to let you know promptly if another writer has gotten in on it ahead of you. Follow up that brief initial query with a more complete proposal in which you indicate the research you plan to do, probable submission date and the overall shape of the piece as you envision it now. Continue to follow developments closely while awaiting reaction to your query. If it's a "hot" story, there's bound to be a market for the piece, whether or not your first query letter uncovers it.

Editors—and therefore, writers—must be aware of the point at which a trend may be on the wane (possibly within the next two or three months), the time when public interest in such subjects as drug abuse, a new diet, solar heating, or a hobby or fad (macramé, CB radios, Vitamin C, biofeedback, behavior modification, group sex or encounter groups, for example), will have been satisfied. Writers should try to avoid coming in on the tag end of a trend that is sure to have produced a flood of article submissions and published articles. With experience—and a study of the subjects found in magazines (to see how far ahead they may have planned articles on the topics included)—you will acquire a "feel" for developing trends and a sense of how much longer they are likely to last. You can then time your articles and queries accordingly.

What to learn from rejections

No writer likes to have a manuscript returned by a magazine, but there are few if any authors who have not had the experience. There are many factors that may lead to a negative decision on a manuscript. You may not be told why the piece was rejected, or, if a reason is given, it may not be the real one. The magazine in question may be cutting back on editorial expenses because of financial reverses. The editor who happens to read your article may have a special prejudice against the subject matter for reasons you have no way of determining. Some people, for example, can't bear stories about Man's Best Friend (there have been so many of them!); others will automatically fall for almost any dog story, no matter how corny. Editors, like other people, have their prejudices and blind spots.

A writer who sold two articles to *The Reader's Digest* phoned me one day to ask why neither one had yet appeared in the magazine. I suggested that she write the managing editor and remind him of the still unpublished manuscripts in the *Digest*'s inventory. "Oh, I wouldn't do that," she groaned. "It's hard enough to submit them in the first place." She added that she had a drawer full of completed pieces she had never sent anywhere, apparently because she couldn't face the possibility that they might be rejected.

This is a completely wrong and self-defeating attitude. There are many reasons for non-scheduling or rejection of a manuscript and not all of them have any relation whatever to the quality of the writing, the importance of the subject, or the writer's skill in presenting his material.

Before you send out an article, make a list of at least three possible markets for it. If it is returned by the first editor, you will then be ready to sit down immediately and address a new envelope to the second market on the list, and then the third. Although you should examine a rejected manuscript carefully for possible clues to reasons for its rejection and ways to improve it, that can wait until the piece has gone out—and bounced back—a few more times.

The readership of the second magazine you query or submit the finished article to may be quite different from the first, and the piece may therefore appeal to a second or third market, though it failed with the first.

If a manuscript does not sell after three or four times out, you should go over it carefully, if possible, objectively, for indicators of what exactly is wrong with it. Think very carefully about any editorial criticism and suggestions for revision offered by editors who reject your work. If proposed changes seem valid to you, make them and resubmit the manuscript with these revisions to the editor who was interested enough to comment constructively.

When a manuscript comes back even after you have revised and rewritten it in line with editorial suggestions and have found some correctable weaknesses, you'll have to decide again whether to query first or to send the article itself. Since it is already written, there's no harm ordinarily in submitting the finished piece (except to a magazine that specifically requires a prior query).

Even if you can't read all the magazines that come out every month—no one could!—it is important to keep in touch with the magazine article market. Regular reading of magazines, noting current tastes and trends they reflect, will suggest ways to refocus and reshape your material, if your first efforts to place it are unsuccessful. Some additional material or a new slant may make the difference. Cutting out extra words and tightening the piece by deleting excessive adjectives and adverbs to make it read more smoothly may do the trick. Today's magazine reader is always in a hurry. Extra verbiage simply irritates the reader, prompting him to switch on his TV set instead.

Don't depend on the editor to do your work for you, although he or she may, if you are lucky, suggest a specific change that will make the piece acceptable.

An article on birding was rejected when first submitted to *The Reader's Digest* on the ground that it "failed to convey to the uninitiated the thrill of the chase, the very real excitement a true birder feels on sighting a new species." The writer took the criticism to heart and rewrote not only the lead paragraph but key parts of the text as well.

Here is the personal lead the author (Marjorie Adams) inserted in the revision of her article:

> About 15 years ago, my husband, Red, upset our lives. He bought me binoculars and Roger Tory Peterson's "A Field Guide to the Birds of Texas." I aimed the binoculars at a bird pecking a hole in a tree, and gasped, "He's so beautiful!" Flipping through Peterson, I found my bird was a red-bellied woodpecker. From that moment, without leaving home, I became a great discoverer. An anonymous brownish wisp became a jaunty Bewick's wren, delivering song wholesale. A pair of Carolina chickadees taught me that birds can be tender. I discovered neighbors I had never met—comical, richly colored green herons.

The author's effort paid off. Upon resubmission, the revised piece was promptly accepted and subsequently published ("Birding—A Sport for All Seasons," *The Reader's Digest,* June 1975).

There are many more examples of article manuscripts that have "gone the rounds" before final acceptance and publication. After sportswriter J. Clayton Stewart's article on hypothermia—the lowering of body temperature to subnormal levels—was turned down by at least three other magazines, he offered it to *Sports Illustrated,* which subsequently published it. Whereupon, *The Reader's Digest* (which he had queried first) picked up the published article for reprinting, giving the author the substantial reprint fee to add to his payment from *Sports Illustrated.*

But even if the author had not hit the jackpot as he did, he would still not have exhausted his options. The subject was of potential interest to readers of a number of magazines. Indeed, an article on hypothermia appeared only a few months later in *WomenSports,* angled a little differently from Stewart's, it's true, but presenting essentially the same set of facts. The same basic material with slightly different treatment might well have sold to any one of the ski magazines and others devoted to outdoor sports.

Literary agents

The beginning article writer does not need a literary agent to sell his manuscripts for him. Most reputable agents, in fact, will not consider taking on a writer until he or she has had a modest body of work published. A simple sale to a magazine is not something one needs an agent to handle. Most magazines have set payment rates, at least for the first few manuscripts purchased from a writer. After that, the rate may be increased, but the decision on that is the magazine's. There is little room for bargaining until a writer reaches professional status, when an agent can be very helpful in arranging subsidiary rights and book sales.

Some well-established writers who have agents still prefer to deal directly with editors when proposing ideas for articles. But in such cases, the agent will discuss the terms, payment, and business arrangements. The check is always sent directly to the agent, who withholds the customary 10% commission and sends the balance to the author.

Submission of manuscripts

There are certain basic procedures that every writer should know before preparing and submitting manuscripts for publication. Failure to follow them can have a negative effect on editors or first readers, marking the writer as an amateur. It is not hard to give your manuscript a professional look so that editors will see that you have learned the accepted requirements of manuscript submission.

Never deliver a manuscript in person. There's no law, of course, against leaving your manuscript in a manila envelope addressed to the editor on the receptionist's desk, but don't succumb to the temptation of trying to visit the editor and hand him or her your manuscript in person. He will not read your piece while you are standing nervously by, and he will be irritated with you for wasting precious time.

Manuscript preparation. Material should be neatly typed, double-spaced on one side of the standard (8½" x 11") typing paper of good quality, leaving ten- to fifteen-space margins. Be sure to include a covering page with the title of the article centered on the page, and your name, address, and telephone number in the lower right-hand corner. It's also a good idea to note the approximate number of words, which should be close to the length of articles generally published in the particular magazine to which you are submitting your article. A moderate amount of additional material and wordage will do no harm and will allow for some cutting and editing, should the article be accepted. Your name only should be typed at the top of each numbered page for identification in case of an office mixup.

Keep carbon copies of everything you submit for publication. It is customary for most magazines to return or report on all full-length article manuscripts that are submitted with self-addressed, stamped return envelopes. But manuscripts do sometimes get lost in the mail or misplaced in transit and it is absolutely essential for writers to keep copies of what they have sent to publishers, so as to have a reference copy in case of loss. Then too, if the manuscript is accepted, the editors may have questions about it or wish to suggest rewriting or revising certain parts. And should a rejected manuscript be lost on its way back to the writer, there will be a copy to Xerox for submission to another publication. *Never send out your only copy.*

Short items often receive different treatment from manuscripts, a fact usually noted on the masthead page (with disclaimers of responsibility for all manuscripts) or in a note with the section that regularly runs this kind of material. Often brief anecdotes, clippings, etc., are not returned to the writer but are destroyed if not accepted, and writers are told to wait a certain length of time before submitting the same material elsewhere.

Self-addressed, stamped envelopes. Despite escalating postal rates, an envelope of proper size for the return of your manuscript should accompany any manuscript or query you submit. Your return address should appear in the upper left-hand corner of the outside envelope. Mailed under the *Special Fourth Class Manuscript Rate,* and so labeled, with letter enclosed (for which first-class postage must be added), the manuscript costs considerably less than first-class mail to send, but service is correspondingly slower.

Payment

How much you are paid for your articles will depend on a number of factors, many of them beyond your control. But since you make the decision on where to submit your manuscript for sale, you should know in advance what your article, if accepted, will bring from that particular market. Not all magazines make information regarding payment public, perhaps because they wish to reserve the right to make such decisions on the basis of the value of an individual piece.

Sometimes writers who receive relatively low payment initially for their articles have their pieces picked up for reprint or condensation or excerpting elsewhere. *The Reader's Digest,* for example, makes a generous reprint payment of $300 per *Digest* page to the author and the same amount to the original publisher—an amount that often exceeds what the author received for the original publication of the article.

~ 14 ~

Practical Pointers

Titles

The title of an article is the first hook you use to attract attention—first, the editor's, then the reader's. Titles are immensely important to the sale of magazines on newsstands and in supermarkets, where a title with real impact can significantly increase sales of a single issue. And, like a good lead (your second hook), a punchy title helps to get the article off to a good start. It should, of course, be related to the subject matter, but not necessarily so directly as to give the story away at the start. Titles should always be as lively and colorful as possible, for they lend interest and excitement to the cover and liven the magazine's pages as the casual reader turns them. Magazine editors spend a good deal of time going over titles, improving or even altogether changing some of them. But the writer who can produce his own catchy titles has an ace in the hole.

Ideas for titles can come from many places. A familiar quote may take on new meaning in connection with an article subject; a slogan or aphorism may, by deft rewording, be made to apply to the article's content. A key line may be pulled from the article's text to serve, in quotes, as the title. An example: In "I'm Not Going," in *Reader's Digest,* the author urges readers to refuse the occasional invitation and spend time at home instead.

Anything that will pique the interest of the reader and at the same time have some connection with the article's content is valid title material. With more than half the population admittedly overweight and many of us chronic dieters, who wouldn't be drawn to an article titled "21 Ways to Lose Weight (*Without* Dieting)," featured on the cover of *New Woman*? "How It Feels to Almost Die," a *Psychology Today* title, may split its infinitive, but it could hardly fail to provoke reader curiosity. *Working Woman* divides what is ordinarily one word to give special meaning to the title "Pants for Every Body." "Blue Collar Polo" suggests, with an admirable economy of words, the new slant on an aristocratic sport that is the theme of this *Yankee* article.

"Wolves in My Bedroom" is a provocative title, though perhaps not so much so to readers of *Alaska Magazine,* in which the piece appeared. But titles need not be either enigmatic or humorous. "The Pill and Cancer: More Tragic Evidence," in *Good Housekeeping,* delivers just what it promises in an article certain to disturb the magazine's large female readership. "When (Not If) the World Runs Out of Oil" is the stark title of an article in *Yankee* that warns of the imminent exhaustion of our petroleum resources. *Organic Gardening* tells "How to Keep Warm for Pennies—Japanese Style." These titles reach out to readers, telling them in a few well-chosen words what the article is about. A catchy title featured on the cover can sell the magazine on the spot to the reader who wants to read that particular article. After scanning the table of contents readers will turn immediately to the page on which a piece with an intriguing title begins. Obviously, not every title can be so compelling. Reader reactions vary according to personal tastes and other factors. Most editors are satisfied to have one or two "hot" titles in an issue. The rest may simply indicate the subject and, when appropriate, the editorial slant of the article.

Variety in the cover listing is achieved through use of the occasional interrogatory title ("Can Vitamins Cure Mental Illness?" "Is Betty Ford Too Frank?" were both on *McCall's* cover. "Is Mars Alive?" was featured on *Saturday Review,* "Who Needs College?" on *Newsweek.*). A *Reader's Digest* table of contents more often than not includes one (but one only) "how to" title ("How to Find a Good Nursing Home," "How to Cope with Jealousy," "How to Get Action When You Complain" are typical), although the issue itself may contain as many as three articles in the same popular category.

Euphony, rhymed words and alliteration are tricks that help make titles stick in the reader's memory. A *Yankee* article on the former Speaker of the House of Representatives was titled "From Andrew Square to the Speaker's Chair"; in *The Atlantic* we find "The Power and the Profits." In *Audubon* such deliberately alliterative headings as "Rapping on Raptors" and "Marine Mammal Muddles" alternate with the challenge of "Will the Bald Eagle Survive to 2076?" and "Kaiparowits—the Ultimate Obscenity."

The "straight" title that simply reveals an article's contents as succinctly as possible still outnumbers others in frequency of use and, if the subject is good, can draw readers just as well. Among titles featured on the cover of *Working Woman's* charter issue were "Love, Honor and Earn—the 2 Income Marriage," "When You Take Your Work to Bed with You," "Good Cooking When You're Too Beat to Bother" and "Jobs: Finding Out What You're Good At"— all designed to catch the eye of the working women this magazine hopes to attract every month.

The promotion department, responsible for newsstand sales, can be counted on to change an enigmatic title when featuring the article on the magazine's cover. The prospective buyer of *Lady's Circle,* for example, would have no doubt about the contents of such articles as these: "Why Your Annual Physical May Not Do Any Good After All" and "Easy Ways to Help Your Children Stop Battling and Start Behaving." And yet the potential purchaser might well be curious about the content of both pieces.

Titles in special-interest magazines also tend to be straightforward and self-explanatory, enabling the informed reader to scan the table of contents quickly for those features that are of particular concern to him. An issue of *Antiques Journal* included the following articles: "Royal Copenhagen Porcelain," "Patriotic Civil War Covers," "Early American Pocket Knives," etc.; *How-to* announces material on how to "Update a Room with Wall Panelings," "Insulate Your Home and Save" and "Pick and Plant a Tree," among other strictly instructional features.

You may or may not have in mind at the outset a title that seems exactly right for your article. If you do have the title you want when you send your query, by all means include it in the letter. It may be just what is needed to sell your idea to an editor. But lack of a really good title need not deter you from sending a query or even an article in otherwise finished form. Editors often retitle articles anyhow, to avoid conflict with other too-similar titles in the same or a recent issue or simply because they think they have a better one. Titles are fair game for editors, who are primarily responsible for the magazine's cover (subject to change by the promotion department as noted above). The editor strives to make the table of contents just as inviting as possible. In the magazines that regularly list titles on the cover, one can assume titles take on added importance. *Harper's* for example, can be counted on for at least one provocative cover title. ("JFK: The King's Pleasure," "Harvard on the Way Down," "Nixon's Night Out" and "Jimmy Carter's Pathetic Lies" enlivened the cover of one particular issue). A *Woman's Day* cover grabs the prospective reader (presumably female) with a full-color picture of luscious chocolate cake, then lures her with such titles as "Yes, You Can Look Prettier" and "Who's Having the Baby? You or the Doctor?" "Signed, Sealed and Devoured" (*Esquire*) and "When Your Love Affair Turns into Marriage" (*Redbook*) pique the reader's curiosity, luring him or her on to buy and read the magazines.

Pay close attention to article titles in your magazine reading. Get into the habit of thinking up your own catchy heads and subheads, jotting them down as they occur to you—before you lose them. Often an idea for a clever title can lead you on to a new subject or a different slant for an article. Never underestimate the power of a title to interest and intrigue both editor and reader, persuading them to read the article itself.

Routines and schedules

Finding time to write is never easy. Most article writers, at least at the start, write part-time and must fit their writing into odd nooks and crannies of their lives while keeping house or earning a living. Some writers rise in the cold light of early dawn and beat the typewriter till breakfast time. (I know one woman who produced her first, quite creditable, novel that way.)

Whatever schedule works best for you, there is real value in setting aside a definite time for writing—one hour of the day, even one morning of the week, when no one, no family crisis, no business obligation can take precedence over that sacred commitment to the typewriter. Subconsciously, the mind works toward that hour, shaping ideas, wording sentences, lining up similes and figures of speech. If all goes well, at the appointed time the words march across the blank pages without too much difficulty. (It was interesting to note, in Thomas Mann's *Letters,* that even so eminent a writer as he had to struggle to guard his three-hour morning work period from interruption and from the continuing temptation to steal time for his always voluminous correspondence.)

There are writers, admittedly, for whom a regular commitment of this sort is wholly incompatible with their temperaments. Such writers must build up to the moment of inspiration and then, sitting at the typewriter for hours on end, work feverishly to set the words down in one great flow of creativity.

The way a writer works is a reflection of individual style and personality, and this is not readily changed. But the effort to establish a writing routine is worthwhile if it can help writers break the habit of procrastination all too common even among established members of the profession. As every writer knows, it is always easy to find other seemingly important things to do. Unless a time is set for writing, one is likely never to get to it.

The common tendency of writers to procrastinate may

stem from a lack of self-confidence that is characteristic of many, even after a degree of success has been achieved. And yet confidence in themselves is what writers need in order to convince first themselves, then editors and finally readers that what they write is worth reading and that their thoughts on a given subject are worthy of attention.

For just this reason, article editors put a great deal of time and effort into building up their writers' self-confidence. This may, in fact, be the editor's most important role vis-à-vis the writers with whom he works on a regular basis.

Typewriters

Every writer should own a typewriter and be able to use it. My own method, which I have found invaluable, may prove useful to others. I type the first draft on inexpensive paper, triple-spacing the text and leaving wide margins to allow for later insertions and corrections. If a sentence doesn't work out, rather than take time to cross it out, I start over. If a paragraph fizzles in the middle, I drop down a line or two on the page and begin another. Surprisingly, this rough text is easy to edit later. It is simple to follow along the right track, crossing out the false starts, rewrites and repetitions.

This is my working copy, to which I make additions in the margins or on the back of sheets. If a change in the order of paragraphs seems desirable, I cut up the page and rearrange it in various ways until I am satisfied that it makes a coherent whole and is ready for final typing.

For the sake of the editors who will read your manuscripts, make sure to keep your typewriter clean and change the ribbon often. There is no question that the manuscript that is accurately and neatly typed on good paper, without visible errors and set up as suggested in the previous chapter, makes a favorable impression on the editor even before he starts to read it. Typewriter correction paper, available at stationery stores, is useful in correcting typing errors.

Writing courses and workshops

If there is a course in magazine article writing being offered at a college or university or in an adult education program near you, taking it could prove worthwhile in your training as a writer. Correspondence courses tend to be more expensive, and, by their very nature, lack the stimulus of classroom give-and-take.

Beginning writers sometimes find writers' conferences and workshops helpful. No matter where you live, you are probably within easy reach of a writers' conference, since there are more than a hundred of them held annually in thirty states, as well as in Canada, Mexico, and Great Britain. Conferences are usually held in the spring or summer, and fees are comparatively modest. Some last one day, others up to two weeks, offering an opportunity for writers to hear and meet successful authors who are willing to share what they have learned about writing for publication. It is encouraging for new writers to meet professionals and comforting to exchange experiences with other neophytes. In the workshop sessions, there is usually constructive criticism of submitted manuscripts and general discussion which is sometimes helpful and always stimulating.

Announcements of writers' conferences appear in local and regional newspapers, and are listed annually in writers' magazines. Many are sponsored by colleges and universities in conjunction with summer programs.

Photographs

For many magazine article writers, a good camera is almost as indispensable as a typewriter. Anything from an inexpensive Instamatic to the more complicated 35 mm. models will produce pictures and transparencies of publishable quality. The better the camera, the sharper and more reproducible the print. Take your camera with you whenever you interview anyone so that you can take pictures if it seems advisable—but only with the permission of the person being interviewed.

The camera is useful in many ways. You'll find that color shots of an unfamiliar scene or color photos of persons you meet and talk with only briefly will help to reconstruct the locale and the people in your mind's eye later, enabling you to include in your text concrete detail that would otherwise have to be either omitted or fabricated. Hair and eye color, the kind of clothes a certain person wore, the breed of dog he had with him or the make of car he drove—these scraps of information might never get into your notebook or impress themselves on your memory in the course of an interview in which your chief concern is, naturally, to record accurately what is said.

Magazines ordinarily pay extra for pictures, and it is a good idea to find out before you do your article (at the query stage) whether the magazine you hope to sell your piece to wants black-and-white glossy prints or color transparencies. If you do not have the equipment or the expertise to provide the kind of pictures a magazine requires, you may be able to find a friend who has.

Tape recorders

Some writers regularly use tape recorders at their interviews (with the permission of the subject, of course); others seem to get bogged down in the large volume of taped material collected in this way and have difficulty sifting through it for what is genuinely significant to the article they are writing. Many writers also make quick notes by hand, as the conversation and taped interview progresses, noting not only what is said, but the manner of speech, and what questions seem to bring the strongest response from the subject, any emotional reactions, physical features, mode of dress, surroundings (if there are some special features about the home or office of the subject), and other points that may later recall or trigger ideas that should be included in the article.

Whether you use a tape recorder or not, type up your notes and transcribe the material on your tapes as soon as possible after the interview. Make sure to include any quotations you were able to get down verbatim. You will find that for a short time after an interview, the details will stay quite clear in your memory.

Your personal reference shelf

Even if there is a well-stocked public library nearby, with a librarian who is unfailingly helpful, there are certain reference works it is well for you to have ready at hand for immediate use. What these are will depend somewhat on the types of articles you write, but these basic reference books are useful to everyone:

A dictionary. The best you can afford. *Webster's New Collegiate,* based on *Webster's Third New International Dictionary* (unabridged) is adequate, but the unabridged is, of course, the best. Keep the desk edition of this dictionary (or one of the others that you may prefer—*Webster's New*

World Dictionary, The American Heritage Dictionary, Random House Dictionary) at hand, but you should consult the unabridged edition frequently, in the library, if necessary. That edition, or one of the other unabridged dictionaries, is a rich sourcebook for any writer. If you have not yet formed the dictionary habit, do so now. There is no excuse for misspellings or slipshod usage in material submitted for publication. Such carelessness can spoil a sale and permanently damage your relations with an editor.

A thesaurus. Most widely used and best known is *Roget's Thesaurus,* in its original subject arrangement or the more modern "dictionary form." This useful tool enables writers to vary their language to express their meaning more precisely and to find the right synonym for a word or phrase in order to avoid repetition. There are other variations of the thesaurus, most recent of which are *The Doubleday Roget Thesaurus in Dictionary Form* and *Webster's Collegiate Thesaurus.*

A style manual. Fowler's *Dictionary of Modern English Usage,* Porter Perrin's *Writer's Guide & Index to English, The Elements of Style* by Strunk and White, *American English Usage, A Dictionary of Usage and Style, The Chicago Manual of Style* are only a few of the volumes that can help you avoid unacceptable word use and bad grammar, and improve your sentence structure.

An almanac. This annual volume provides important, up-to-date information on a wide range of subjects and is invaluable for quickly checking facts that require authentication. There are several to choose from— *The World Almanac, Information Please Almanac,* for example—and you may want to own more than one.

The Reader's Encyclopedia. A tremendously useful literary reference volume. It covers all aspects of modern and classical literature, as well as selected items on invention and science, history, authors, books, stories, background facts, and an impressive range of material found almost nowhere else. An especially worthwhile volume for writers to own.

The Columbia Encyclopedia. An expensive, but very useful one-volume encyclopedia which helps writers check many points of fact without special trips to the library.

Bartlett's Familiar Quotations and *The Oxford Dictionary of Quotations.* The most important volumes of this kind, though there are others of more specialized nature that individual writers may have special use for in their article writing.

Ploetz' Manual of Universal History. A remarkable compilation of historical information. It has not been revised for some time, and its current sections are therefore not up-to-date. But it remains one of the handiest historical reference books available because of its format and the vast range of world events that it covers, all in one small volume.

Telephone books. A local phone book, along with the Yellow Pages, is useful. If you can obtain one (the phone company will usually supply a copy on request), the directory for the nearest metropolitan area is good to have, too. If you spend your vacations regularly in another part of the country, make sure to bring home a phone book from there, again one with the Yellow Pages if possible. Phone books are carefully edited and serve as reliable guides to the correct spellings of the names of persons and places. The Yellow Pages are useful for leads they may contain—to unique businesses and services in your area, for example, or to indicate, from the number of listings, business trends you might not otherwise notice.

The Writer's Handbook. Finally, for ready reference to market information and much other useful data as well, you will want to keep at hand the most recent edition of *The Writer's Handbook,* edited by A. S. Burack.

Each writer can also decide what other reference books may be most useful for special fields and keep those at hand in addition to these "basic" volumes. Your reference library will undoubtedly grow from year to year as you acquire volumes needed in connection with articles you are developing.

One last word

To those of you who occasionally suffer from lack of confidence in your work and are crushed by rejections when, as inevitably they must, they come to you, let me say simply, "Take heart." Chances for the new writer to break into the magazine field today are better than they ever were. There are more article markets now than ever before, and editors are actively seeking new writers who are reliable and know their craft. A well-written, carefully researched article on a timely subject can hardly fail to find acceptance, even if, for a variety of possible reasons, the manuscript is returned the first—or even the tenth—time it goes out. *Keep trying.*

Don't be discouraged if your article doesn't sell to one of the big-circulation magazines. As you have seen, there are literally hundreds of smaller markets to try.

The first markets you approached may already have similar material scheduled or in inventory or have commitments to other writers on subjects close to yours. Before sending the manuscript out again, take another look at it to see if there is a section you can strengthen, a paragraph that drags.

A few pages can be quickly retyped and repaged and the manuscript will be ready for another trip. The extra work and effort you put into it will very likely pay off.

Careful research and meticulous attention to the actual writing will help you find markets for your work, even though competition is keen. The writing must be lively and readable, must reflect the considerable effort that went into it. These are not unreasonable demands and there is no need to be intimidated by them. When you are satisfied that you have produced a creditable piece of work on a subject that will interest a substantial number of readers, send the manuscript out. If it comes back, send it out again—and again and again, if necessary, remembering that only you keep a record of your rejections.

While you are anxiously awaiting the final disposition of that first article, don't just sit idle. The time will pass quickly if you are thinking about, working on, taking notes for and planning your next piece. While waiting, you can be doing your research and preparing a query proposing a new article subject. Perhaps you will already have an encouraging letter from an editor on the new piece before you hear about that first submission. Whatever the verdict on it is, be assured that, as time goes on, disappointments will be fewer, acceptances more frequent. You may find you are working harder than ever, working and learning, for successful writing involves a great deal of both. That's what makes it the satisfying occupation it is.